This book is dedicated
to my husband, Red, and our
daughter, Sarah,
dear companions on the journey.

I should like to express my appreciation to Louis D. Rubin, Jr., who got rid of the detours and taught me the beauty of the straight line; and to Dr. William W. Rogers, Professor of History at Florida State University, who read the early manuscript, liked it, and said, "Keep on writing."

of these changes, and I think the telling of them can be interesting. I have discovered not only that writing is good therapy but that it also can be an ego trip.

Why did I want to write this book? I felt a need to say "thank you" to friends who have shared the good days and the rough times. I wanted to pay tribute to the gallant women of my ancestry who endured the hardships of the Civil War and Reconstruction and survived with strength and grace.

Most of all, I want my daughter, Sarah, to know where she came from, who, and what she is.

This book—and in important ways my life—is divided into three parts. Part One is set in the South of my early years. I wanted to tell not only of my own experience of growing up in North Florida, but also about my family and a way of life that, as I look back from the vantage point of almost eighty years, seems as though it took place in another world, so different were its rhythms and its cadences. The South when I was growing up was still very much a part of the small-town and rural nineteenth century from which it was slowly and painfully emerging. So much has changed since then that sometimes it is difficult to realize that I was once a part of it and knew it for reality. I wanted to preserve something of what it meant to live in that time and place.

Part Two—"North"—tells of my abrupt dislodgement from that early life, and a sometimes near breathless adventure in modern urban life as I followed my husband's fortunes as a baseball broadcaster and active personality in the American sports scene.

Part Three is the story of my return to a place and time different from the Florida I had known as a child. Yet I was not a stranger. I was home again. It is a time and a place for rest and refreshment before the traveler resumes her journey.

Tallahassee, Florida   LYLAH BARBER
June 30, 1984

. . . that among all the changes and chances
of this mortal life . . .

*from the original Book of
Common Prayer, 1549 . . .
based on an ancient Collect
of a mass for travelers.*

MY FATHER

I was born in Lake City, Florida, July 7, 1906, at three in the afternoon in a house one block from my grandmother's home. My mother was two weeks past her twenty-first birthday, and my father, after having "read the Law" in Colonel Henderson's office in Tallahassee, was just beginning to practice. When I was quite small I was told that later in the day on which I was born, he came home from town with a bouquet of roses and a new dress for my mother, and a little gold ring with a tiny diamond for me. My parents named me Lylah for my mother and Murray for my father. A few months later we moved to Jacksonville, where my father went into law practice with his brother Maurice. My brother Mat was born there when I was a year-and-a-half old.

What was he really like—this handsome young man whom I loved so much? The framed picture I have of him with the dark hair and haunting eyes in a young slender face gives him more the look of a poet than a lawyer. He was my first love! I think my earliest memory is of my father's arms riding me high on his shoulders—from there I surveyed my world and found it very good. He would take me with him on neighborhood errands. Those trips became part of a very special sort of world with just the two of us living in it. At that time we lived in Jacksonville in a house on the street-car line. I remember running after him when he would leave for the office, crying, "Take me, take me!" The day he went to the hospital is still vivid in my memory. He wore a long opera-type coat and a hat pulled down over one eye. It was raining and the house seemed very dark. I was crying and holding on to him when the horse and buggy came to take him. In the doorway he turned to me and said, "Don't cry, little Murray, when I come back I will buy you a pony and a cart." He never came back.

I do not actually know what caused my father's death, but do seem to remember someone saying "intestinal tuberculosis," whatever

Father, shortly before his marriage.

that may have meant. Certainly tuberculosis was a common enough ailment among young adults of that time. He did have weeks of hospitalization for which the bills must have been overwhelming.

My maternal grandmother, whom we called Dannie, took my brother and me to the house where she and Aunt Ouida—my mother's younger sister—lived, and we stayed with them while Mother took my father's body back to Lake City for burial. I remember missing my mother and wondering where she was. When she finally returned, dressed all in black, I was frightened. I had never seen her like that before. I was afraid to go to her—she seemed a stranger. It was September and the day was hot. Dannie helped Mother out of the black dress, and she lay on the bed in her slip and cried. People kept me away from her and I grew more frightened. That is the only time I ever saw my mother cry.

For years, all through my childhood, my young adulthood and into my marriage, I was plagued by a recurrent nightmare. I would awaken sobbing in terror and drenched with sweat. In the dream there was a small white cottage built on brick stilts enclosed by wooden lattice work. The house was in a desolate marsh-like area covered with a kind of saw grass. Sometimes I was in the marsh being terribly cut by the grass and unable to escape. In other dreams I was in the house. It was always the same—only empty dusty rooms—except that sometimes there was a too-tall dark man of whom I was dreadfully afraid. In one corner of the largest room a wooden coffin stood upright.

How puzzled my young husband must have been the first time he was awakened by my screams of terror. However, he was kindly patient and over a number of years we worked out the reasons for my recurring nightmare. When I finally could recall that the house was the one my father left—to which he never returned—and that the dark man was the driver of the carriage that took him away, the terror vanished and only the sadness of loss remained.

I loved and still love my father so much. Growing up, how I envied my girl friends, whose fathers were living; the close relationship, the exciting treats provided by the indulgent male parent—all

My father, Lindley Murray Scarborough, in military school uniform.

were missing and so missed by me. I was only two months past my fifth birthday when he died, and my actual memories of him are, of necessity, few and dim.

However, over the years, his contemporaries, relatives, and friends who outlived him filled in pieces from their memories, and the mosaic grew. The photograph of Murray Scarborough, the handsome young lawyer, which I cherish was given to me by a patient, Mr. Lewis Lively, when I was a student nurse at Riverside Hospital in Jacksonville. Mr. Lively was from Tallahassee and had been a friend of my father's when he was living there and studying law in Colonel Henderson's office.

When I was nineteen I came to Tallahassee to attend Florida State College for Women. I met a number of people who had known my father, and the picture of him grew. I inherited his dark hair and eyes and have been told I look very much like him. I suppose I do, for I was asked several times by strangers, "Are you Murray Scarborough's child?" It gave me much delight to say, "Yes." The "Argyle Sisters," maiden ladies who rented rooms to "certain young gentlemen," had me to tea and told me how much they enjoyed having had my father in their home. Mrs. Sadie Henderson, who was daughter-in-law of the colonel in whose office my father had read the law, and about the age my father would have been, had me to family dinner one Sunday after church, and there were more stories.

When my husband and I came to Tallahassee to retire, some forty-five years later, Miss Sadie was still living. A college friend of mine took me calling. She was a very old lady then and confined to her home and a wheelchair, but she was dressed for the occasion and was most gracious. I am not sure that she really remembered me, but she remembered, very well, the young man with the dark hair and eyes!

A final piece to complete the picture; this comes to me from my aunt Ouida. My father was visiting, shortly after his marriage, with his mother and was heard to say, "But Mama, Lyla doesn't know how to cook anything." Grandma was quick to reply, "Now Murray, you could have married one of those suitable women of your own age, but you wanted the pretty young girl, so just get busy and make

enough money for her to have a cook." Not much sympathy from
that realist. And my mother never learned to cook.

In 1946 when Edward R. Murrow, the great CBS broadcaster of
World War II and the McCarthy era, returned from his wartime
years in England, he became vice-president in charge of news and
special events for the CBS network. By then my husband and I were
living in New York and he was broadcasting the Brooklyn Dodgers
baseball games. Murrow hired Red Barber to be his director of
sports, succeeding Ted Husing, who had quit.

When I met Murrow I was amazed. He looked just like the cherished picture of my father as a young man. Like my father he was a
Southerner with the charm and courtly manners that I am certain my
father had. We became friends with Ed and his wife Janet.

When Murrow died in 1965 at age fifty-seven, St. James Church
on 71st and Madison Avenue was filled with the great and the hum-
ble for his funeral service. When I came home from the church, I
could not hold back the tears. I cried for the loss of a friend, and the
death of a giant in my husband's profession.

I realized also that I wept for the father whose loss I had been too
young to fully understand. Somehow the tears for Murrow helped
heal a grief that came into the cottage when my father died in 1911,
leaving a young widow and two small children. I was five and my
brother Mat was three.

MY GRANDMOTHER'S HOUSE

The house which holds so many of my early childhood memories was in the small North Florida town of Lake City. A large two-story white house, it sat in its garden alone on the block except for a bank building which occupied one corner and was known to me simply as Uncle Fred's bank. In truth it was, for he was both owner and president. The little building with its white Greek columns still stands, but it now houses a jewelry and gift shop.

There was a fountain in the front yard of Grandma Scarborough's house. On hot summer days I was allowed to wade and splash in it. There were fig trees I climbed, and when the fruit was ripe I picked it for Grandma to make preserves. The house itself was L-shaped with the short arm facing the street and the long one running back into the garden. There were front porches and back porches both upstairs and down. All the rooms seemed large to me, and there were many of them. Downstairs there were the parlor, the dining room, the kitchen, and Grandma's bedroom. Upstairs were what seemed to me a vast number of bedrooms. I guess there were, too, for six children had been born and all but one raised to adulthood in that house. Part of the upstairs back porch had been converted into a modern bathroom.

But the heart of the house was Grandma. I was five when my father died, and I began spending much of my school vacation time in Lake City with Grandma. In the summer a morning glory vine shaded the front porch and shut out some of the hot sun. In the evening the light from the lamp on the street corner filtered through and looked like moonlight. It made a very private world just for Grandma and me. She would hold me in her lap and rock me, and sing the sad and romantic songs of the Civil War in which all the girls were young and beautiful, and the men were brave, going off to the War to fight for their Land. Sometimes Grandpa would sit on the

Grandma and Grandpa Scarborough.

front steps, but mostly it was just Grandma and me. I would fall
asleep, and it must have been he who carried me to bed.

Grandpa was a thin man with piercing black eyes and a salt-and-
pepper moustache and beard. He was a quiet man who obviously
adored his exuberant, plump Fanny, and I never heard him raise his
voice to her. Once in a while he would venture a gentle, "Now,
Fanny." For many years he was Clerk of the Court. When the courthouse closed for lunch he would come home for the heavy hot mid-
day dinner that was customary. On summer afternoons, when the
watermelons were ripe, he would occasionally arrive early for a special treat for me and whatever neighborhood children were handy.
When a bell announced the approach of the black watermelon man
and his wagon of melons, Grandpa would take me by the hand and
out we would go. There would be much thumping and inspecting
until the perfect choice was made. Then we climbed up on the
wagon and rode to the icehouse where our prize would be left to

cool. There always seemed to be a cold one, chosen the day before, waiting to be brought back home to be cut at the table on the back porch and grabbed by eager hands and devoured. One melon cut lengthwise served four children. Then followed the contest to determine who could spit the black seeds the farthest. The rinds were carefully saved for Grandma to make her wonderful pickles. In fact, the summer seemed to proceed in an orderly fashion, beginning with the preserving of figs, moving on to brandied peaches and watermelon pickles, then to a sort of chow-chow of cabbage, red and green peppers and onions and *lots* of spices. Finally there was the grand finale of preserved little pears called, I think, "sickle."

At the time of my visits the only one of my grandparents' six children who remained at home was Aunt Lora. She had been born late into her parents' lives after the others were teenagers and young adults, and her older sister and brothers had petted and spoiled her! She was probably about eighteen years old then, and it fell her duty, most unwillingly, I suspect, to take me to Sunday service at the little Episcopal church where my mother and father had been married. She would quickly drop me at the door and go about her young-girl business. To my delight I found myself sitting up in the chancel with the choir—why, I can't imagine, since I was and am a perfect monotone. Perhaps Mr. Cavell, the rector, felt I was less lonely there. Many years later when my daughter Sarah, then a college student at Rollins, in Winter Park, Florida, and I were driving back to our home in New York we detoured by Lake City and I took her to the church. "But Mother, it's so tiny," she said. And so it was. But it hadn't seemed so to me when I was five years old. When I returned to Lake City recently it still looked the same, a fresh coat of white paint the only difference.

On rainy days when I couldn't play outside, Grandma was full of the most surprising ways to help pass the time. I remember being allowed to play with her long thick hair. She would sit before her dressing table and let me comb and braid and arrange her hair in various fashions. Since my own hair was very straight and worn very short, this game was quite a treat. When I tired of the game it was she, of course, who had to brush out the snarls, and what a job that must have been! Another rainy day we removed the crystal prisms from the chandelier in the parlor. They were then washed in ammonia water and dried. I was allowed to stand on a table and rehang them. How they sparkled in the light. Pretty smart, this grandma!

But that's not the only time Grandma was smart. One summer Cousin Lily Mae came visiting with her infant daughter. Lily Mae's mother had died when she was young and Grandma had cared for her often, as she now, years later, cared for me. The baby Imogene was still bottle-fed, and every morning those bottles had to be washed and then filled with raw rice and water and shaken hard. That was my special privilege. Imogene is now the wife of a distinguished federal judge, and it sometimes amuses me to remember that one summer I was her number-one bottle washer.

Then there were the stories of the Indians. The Indian War was over by August, 1842. However, when Grandma was a young girl growing up on a plantation in the White Springs area, there were still pockets of more or less friendly Indians living nearby who had not been sent to the reservations. I would beg, "Tell me about the honey." The tribal chief and his warriors often came to visit her father. They would sit in a circle in the yard and pow-pow. One day the chief appeared with his men and a gift, a freshly killed cow's skull filled with wild honey, which was passed around the circle. Everyone dipped two fingers into the honey and licked. To have refused would have been an insult and might have precipitated strained relations.

Some afternoons following a post-dinner nap and bath, we would put on our "calling on" clothes and go to see Cousin Kate. We always took a gift, often fresh figs in a little basket which I carried. This walk was quite long—across town, over the railroad tracks (that's how I learned the expression "on the other side of the tracks"), and down a country lane to a large house, sort of a farm house, with a vegetable garden and a playground with swings. There were children there, and I was left to play with them in the yard while Grandma visited with "Poor Kate." I never saw her. I still

Lylah, at about three years of age.

wonder whether she had retreated to an upstairs bedroom a chronic invalid, the victim of too many children too quickly and primitive obstetrical care, as did many Southern women of that time, or had just become a little "queer" but was decently and patiently kept in her own home, as was also the custom of the times. I never found out, but I was repeatedly and pointedly told, "She's not really your blood kin." Nevertheless, sometimes when I react in a peculiar fashion I think some of Cousin Kate rubbed off on me.

Speaking of playmates, I was always allowed to play with the black cook's children, who often accompanied their mother when she came to work, but never with those of a certain family in the neighborhood because they were "poor white trash." Oh, Grandma had her tough side too, and once when I disobeyed and ran away to satisfy my curiosity about them, I was punished by being banished to my room for the rest of the afternoon.

There also was my cousin Jessie, the daughter of Aunt Ruby, my father's sister, and Uncle Fred Cone, who owned the bank. Jessie lived nearby, but we seldom played together because she was three years older—and at six and nine the gulf is wide and deep. Aunt Ruby played the piano and sang and was said to have been "the most beautiful young lady in Lake City." Willful she certainly was. Walking home one day she passed the livery stable and stopped to watch a fight. A young man, a stranger to her, was taking on and defeating all challengers. Arriving home she announced to her mother, "I've just seen the strongest man in the world and I'm going to marry him." And marry him she did. It was not a very happy union, and she died when her only child, Jessie, was about fifteen or sixteen. Perhaps the strong young stranger was too strong for the spoiled beauty. He certainly was colorful.

Fred Cone became a dominant figure in the economic and political life of Lake City and the state, and the stories about him are legend. One of my favorites is the one about when President Roosevelt closed the banks in the Great Depression. They stayed closed for three days, and apprehension spread among the depositors in Uncle Fred's bank. Mildred, his second wife, told me the story of what happened when the banks reopened. He and Mildred made the trip to Jacksonville early on the morning of the day the banks were to reopen, to borrow the money to have in reserve should there be a run on the bank. Word spread quickly that the bank was going to open, and a long line of depositors formed outside demanding that the doors open so they could "get their money." Federal marshals stood on either side of the closed doors, holding the crowd back. Suddenly the doors did open, and there stood Uncle Fred. He announced in a loud voice, "These people are my friends, their money is safe, and if

My brother Matthew, called Mat.

they want it I'm going to give it to them. Don't anybody try to stop me." I have heard it told that he backed up his words with a shot-gun. I don't really know about that, but after the first depositors closed their accounts and were paid in full, people began to drift away. The crisis was over. The bank was sound and so it remained.

Years later when Uncle Fred was Governor Cone, the story is told that one of his aides warned him, in rather pungent tones, about the questionable loyalty of one of his patronage appointees. "Fred," he said, "You ought to get rid of him; he's a no-good son of a bitch." To this advice Uncle Fred replied, "Yes, I know, but he's my son of a bitch, and you leave him alone."

After my father's death, Mother had a hard struggle to keep her head above water. Uncle Fred was helpful and even offered to take my three-year-old brother to be raised as his and Aunt Ruby's son. Mother was sorely tempted. Times were terribly hard, and if she were to accept the offer, Mat would have all the advantages money could bring. There was a condition attached to Uncle Fred's offer. Mat would have to be legally adopted, and his name would be changed to Cone. Finally, Mother could not agree to such terms. What Uncle Fred wanted, understandably, was a son to bear his name. The beautiful young girl he married had become a chronic invalid and spent most of her days in bed upstairs. She would never give him the son he desired. Mother was wise. My gentle, vulnerable brother could never have become the son that ambitious, hard-driving man wanted.

I am glad she saw to it that Mat kept his dead father's name. His daughter, Mary Anne, whom he loved dearly, is so proud of her Scarborough name. Mat died when she was only seven. Mary Anne married Michael O'Donnell, and named her son Philip Scarborough O'Donnell.

My own daughter too is proud of her heritage and sometimes says, only half in jest, that when she has a little extra money she is going to have the Scarborough name added legally, after the Spanish fashion, to her own. Since she is already Sarah Lanier Barber, that will be quite a mouthful. Her paternal great-grandmother was a Lanier and cousin to the poet Sidney Lanier.

After Grandpa died, Grandma came to Jacksonville to live with her son, my uncle Maurice, who at that time was still a bachelor. Aunt Lora came with her, and Mother and Mat and I moved in as well. We lived in the downstairs of an apartment house in the Springfield section of town, and things were pretty crowded. The arrangement was short-lived, as this was about the time Mother was finally able to purchase the little house in which we lived with Dannie until Mother's remarriage, and my memories of that time are few. Mostly I remember Grandma's cooking. The kitchen had an old-fashioned wood-burning stove with a warming apron. She would french-fry potatoes and put them on a platter on the warmer. I stood by and ate them as quickly as she cooked, and she would pretend she didn't see. When the figs and guavas were ripe, she made fresh fruit ice cream, and Mat and I would churn the freezer. As a reward we were given the dasher to lick. Her ice cream was the rich, boiled-custard type.

When we were older and living with my stepfather, my brother and I, on Sunday afternoons, were sent across town to visit Grandma, who by then was an old lady and not very well. We were given money for the streetcar fare. I regret to say we would cut our visits short and spend the nickels to go to the picture show and then walk home. I still have not decided whether the visits to Grandma were kindness on the part of my stepfather, or a desire to get us out of the house for the afternoon.

Grandma died the year I was a senior at St. Joseph's Academy in Jacksonville. Aunt Lora, Uncle Maurice, and I made the journey with her back to Lake City. She lies there with Grandpa and my father, her first son, on one side, and Daisey, the little girl who died in infancy, on the other. The remaining four of her six children are buried with the families into which they married.

Grandma, whose maiden name was Charles, was third generation Columbia County. (This makes me fifth generation.) Family tradition has it that the first Charles came from England around 1815–20 with a group of settlers bound for Virginia. He brought with him his wife Rebecca. The ship they were on was blown off course by a storm, and they landed at St. Augustine. Tradition also says that their daughter Drucilla was the first white child born in St. Augustine after the flag of the United States was raised there in 1821. Records show her as the great-grandmother of Imogene, whose bottles I so laboriously scrubbed. I have not been able to find much about the early days of the Charles family. The courthouse in Lake City suffered a disastrous fire and there are gaps, but the census records of 1850 show this:

Charles—Rebecca F. 50 $1,000—over 20 yrs. cannot read or write
        Drucilla 27 F
        Mary   22 F
        Reuben   15 M.

Poor Rebecca, another widow and illiterate. However, ten years later, in 1860, the same census tells us:

Charles, Reuben   merchant—Real estate
                  $1500 Personal estate $7,000

He is now 27, educated, and the father of my grandma. Cold, impersonal figures? Not for me.

THE WOMEN ENDURED

My father's death set my life into an almost completely matriarchal existence. The bitter cycle of a husband's death leaving the widow to raise small children continued for the third straight time in my family. It was not only my family's pattern; it also was a familiar pattern of the destinies of Southern women, destinies shaped by the Civil War, by the defeat of the Confederacy, by the bitterness of Reconstruction, and by the hard years that followed.

Minerva, then her daughter Florence, and then her daughter Lyla, my mother—one generation after another. Marriage, children, death, and years of endless work. These three women were different in temperament but alike in purpose. They shared a common strength, a determination to survive, and a fierce pride. They knew who they were, what they had to do. Through it all they refused to compromise their moral and cultural standards. They were strong women. They saw it through. They had no time for tears.

Minerva, my great-grandmother, died at the age of seventy-eight when I was two years old. My brother and I never called her daughter, Florence, who was our grandmother, by any other name than Dannie. My mother was named Lyla. I too am a Lylah, but with a different spelling.

Minerva, as far as I can tell from early Columbia County census records, came to Florida from the town of Social Circle, which is in Middle Georgia. The exact year is uncertain, but it was around 1853. She was twenty-four years old. Her husband, Clarke D. Parks, was twenty-three years her senior. Minerva was his second wife. The couple had an infant son, John. While studying the birth records in the Parks family Bible I discovered that Minerva was the sixth of ten children. Her mother had a baby every two years, regular as clockwork. My paternal grandmother had her last baby when she was almost fifty years old. Large families were the usual pattern.

Minerva and Clarke brought with them, by wagon and mule team, all their household goods, furniture and clothing. The furnishings amounted to quite a lot since by then they had been married almost five years. It must have been a hard journey. Perhaps some sort of house anticipated their arrival, or maybe they stayed with other planters while their own home was being built. Did the slaves come with them or were they bought afterward at the market in St. Augustine? I know that at the time of my great-grandfather's death there were twenty-four of them. The faded account book with the inventory of his estate lists them by name and skill. It also gives the value of a mule as greater than that of a human being. When in some shock I pointed this out to Dannie, my grandmother who was Minerva's child, she explained, "Of course, with a mule you could plow, plant food, and eat."

My great-grandfather Clarke died in 1864 in the closing days of the war. He left Minerva, then only thirty-four, with five children. They ranged in age from John, eleven, to Florence, my grandmother, still a babe in arms. A second son, Kendall, had died when he was less than two years old. Minerva was two months pregnant when her husband died. He also left her some 1,500 acres of land, but there was no way to make it productive. No slaves remained to work the fields.

Two years after her husband's death Minerva married George Hancock, who had been the plantation overseer before and during the war. She bore him a son, George, and a daughter, Hattie. I never heard Dannie mention that she had a halfbrother and a halfsister. I don't believe Mother knew it, either, but there they are on the 1870 census—silent witnesses to Dannie's lifelong hatred of her stepfather. Both George and Hattie died in infancy.

The account book, statistical but poignant, which chronicles so much of what I write about contains a vivid picture of 1865, the year of defeat and hunger. A note appears at the end of the estate's legal appraisal that followed the death of my great-grandfather. It reads: "The meat, corn, fodder and potatoes were used for the support of the family. Twenty-four negroes were to be fed until they were set at Liberty—they stole a portion of the bacon."

George Hancock, the stepfather, became legal guardian of the six minor Parks children. He kept a meticulous account of his stewardship. Renting of the land in small parcels to tenant farmers was begun. Later, it would be sold in the same way. The tax rolls tell the story:

1859 –1400 acres
1869 – 280 acres

The pre-war plantation way of life had vanished in a single decade.

Dannie—Florence, my mother's mother—was born during the Civil War on June 24, 1863. It was a time too late to know the prosperity of the plantation era and too early to escape the privation of Reconstruction. She was next to the last of the six Parks children. Her father died before she could remember him. Dannie never quite forgave her mother Minerva for marrying the man who had been her father's plantation manager. Dannie said of her mother, "She married beneath her," but I have a feeling George Hancock was a lifesaver for the widow with six children.

I can't recall how young I was when I first became acquainted with the account book that holds notarized records, beginning in the year 1844. That was when great-grandfather Clarke D. Parks was named executor for the estate of a certain Mr. E. Kendall. The book ends in 1878 with a bill of sixty-five dollars for clothing and forty dollars for board (maybe school in town?) for Florence, my grandmother. I'm sure Dannie kept the account book, because she lived and died firmly convinced that some day the federal government would make compensation for the slaves that had been freed. When I married she gave it to me for safekeeping. It was in my hands until 1979 when, fearing fire or some other accident, I gave it to the Florida State Library in Tallahassee. I felt pretty sure the government wasn't going to compensate me for those slaves.

The records kept of prices of services and commodities by Mr. Hancock would be an economic historian's delight. Minnie, the

My grandmother, Dannie (*center*), with her daughters Lyla, my mother
(*left*), and Ouida (*right*).

posthumous child who died when four years of age, appears in the
records only twice: once for the payment of a small clothing bill, and
then in 1868 there is the notation, "burial for Minnie $4.50." Poor
Minnie. I never knew until I began my research that she had ever
lived. Her sister, my Dannie who told me so many stories of the past,
never mentioned her name. She must have resented the new baby
who took her place in her mother's attentions.

About Mary, an earlier child who died in May, 1871, there appear
the following entries:

> May 25th to A Peeler M.D. for visits and
> attendance $10
>
> May 27th to R. L. Pritchard for making
> coffin for Mary Parks $7

and finally

> to Jas. E. Young for articles for burial
> of Miss Mary Parks $9.93.

The whole life of Mary, aged sixteen, is encapsulated in three notes
in a plantation account book.

There are many notations of the tuition fees paid for all the children. I was told by Dannie that it was customary for the teacher to live at the home of one of the area's planters. The various neighborhood children were brought there for classes. Later the older ones were boarded in Lake City during the week to attend the town school. Certainly the education was rudimentary, but they learned to read and write and "do figures." There were books everywhere. The Anglo-American settlers of North Florida brought the English classics with them. I remember particularly an enormous volume of John Milton's *Paradise Lost* with beautiful engraved illustrations. The book was so heavy that I could not hold it. I had to sit in a chair, at a table, to turn the pages. Most of the books gradually disappeared with the numerous moves the family made during my childhood, but the fire they kindled in me still burns.

One of the tutors (or perhaps he taught in the academy Dannie attended later in town) was a young man from Georgia named George Watts. The son of a Methodist preacher, he and his young pupil fell in love and were soon married. That Dannie was then not quite sixteen must have distressed her mother. They were married New Year's Day, 1871; I wonder if they ran away? They moved into Lake City, and there three children were born. The first child was a boy who died when he was ten months old. The young mother, barely twenty-one herself, grieved excessively; and when my mother was born a year later, she could not accept and be comforted by the healthy little girl. Somehow Mother became partly responsible for the boy's death. So began the bitter lifelong love-hate relationship between my grandmother and my mother. Instead of abating, the conflict grew through the years and crippled them both. (It was severed only by Dannie's death at age eighty-seven.) Three years after Mother's birth Aunt Ouida was born, and she became and remained the beloved child. Aunt Ouida was warm, gay, loving. She and Mother were devoted sisters. Aunt Ouida had no children of her own, and my brother Mat and I shared her with the stepchildren she raised. Aunt Ouida supplied much of the joy and fun of our childhood.

Dannie's children were still young, aged four and one, when her husband died. He went hunting with friends one cold, rainy day, stayed wet from dawn until darkness, came home, and developed pneumonia.

Three generations of widows in my family were left with small children to raise alone, thus exemplifying the matriarchal society that still existed in the South when I was young. These were strong women who needed and found the resourcefulness to survive.

There was Minerva, who married the overseer after her first husband died. She brought only four of the nine children she bore to adulthood. I often wonder what happened to Mary, who died when sixteen. Was it diphtheria, the great killer of children in the days before immunization? Was it typhoid, which was still epidemic in the South when I was a student nurse many years later? (My mother had typhoid when she was carrying my brother Mat.) Perhaps there was an accident—maybe while riding a horse?

Then there was Dannie, who as a child would have been taught "hand work"—plain sewing, embroidery, knitting, and crochet. She became by widow's necessity a fine dressmaker. I remember watching her make a wedding gown of white satin, trimmed with lace and embroidered with seed pearls. I was allowed to watch while the young bride-to-be was "fitted."

On special occasions she made clothing for me. When I was graduated from high school at St. Joseph's Academy in Jacksonville she made me a white organdy dress with lace panels. That was an award for being class valedictorian. When I was working at the University of Florida Infirmary, where I had met the student I was later to marry, Dannie made a red "point-d'esprit" evening dress to wear to the military ball, the big social event of the campus year. For my trousseau she made me a pale pink nightgown trimmed with marabou, a sort of feathery material fashionable at the time. When I discovered that there was a small pocket in the gown and asked why, I was told, "Why for your mad money, of course, child." Once, when I was older, I asked her what became of her share of her father's estate. Her response was quick and bitter. She said, speaking of her husband, the preacher's son, "He spent it all on fast women and slow horses." Poor Dannie, she carried such a heavy load of bitterness and hate.

When Mat and I were small and Dannie was busy looking after us while Mother worked, there were two small stools, one on either side of her sewing machine. If we misbehaved, we were punished by being made to sit quietly on them for a certain length of time. If we talked that added more minutes to the time.

I think I was always aware of the conflict between my mother and Dannie, her mother. Even in the years they shared the same house, when Dannie took care of us and Mother went to work, my brother and I sensed the tension. I do not recall a sharp word being exchanged between them, yet even now I remember the incident of the homespun bed coverlet. It had belonged to Mother's grandmother, Minerva, and had been woven by slaves on the Parks' plantation. Mother and her grandmother had been close, and Minerva gave Mother the coverlet, perhaps as a wedding present. It covered her bed in the cottage she was buying and which we shared with Dannie. It must have been an unpleasant surprise when Mother came home one night and discovered that Dannie had decided to use it as a rug on the living room floor. If there was an exchange of words, neither my brother nor I heard it, but the sense of a battle being drawn lingered in the air.

The routine of those early years when Mother lived and shared expenses with various female kin must have been bewildering to a small child, but I don't recall ever questioning the situation. There was a certain constancy. Mother's working hours were long. She was often gone by the time we were awake and eating breakfast and seldom returned before we were in bed for the night. There were few shared meals. I know that Mother often augmented her salary as a private secretary by filling in upon occasion for the public stenographer in the leading hotel in Jacksonville. She was so young in those hard years, in her late twenties and early thirties, and pretty, too. I expect she shared meals with other young people in the same circumstances.

Dannie also worked from time to time in Cousin Joe Young's General Merchandise Store in Lake City. In those harsh days the sense of family was dominant. One member's fortune or disaster became the joy or sorrow of all. Still evident in the South of today is a strong sense of "blood kinship." I have only two close kin left: my daughter, Sarah, and my brother's child, Mary Anne, who was, until her marriage, the last to bear the Scarborough name. I find myself thinking, "This table must go to Sarah—it was made on her great-great-grandmother Minerva's plantation and Sarah loves beautiful furniture," or, "I will give Mary Anne her great-great-grandmother's cameo necklace, as she is a jewelry girl."

Without Dannie I don't know what would have happened during those early childhood years when Mother had to "go to business" to bring in the money that kept us going. She made it possible for us to stay together at home. There were no day-care centers for working mothers in those days.

As I have become more involved in the research needed in the writing of this book my respect for my pioneer ancestors has grown enormously. It took courage and a sense of adventure for Minerva to leave the established plantation life at Social Circle, Georgia, and head for the undeveloped frontier of North Florida with her husband and infant son. It meant leaving behind friends and family and starting from scratch with only what they had come seeking—fertile unexhausted land. Medical care was almost nonexistent. There were few doctors, and they were poorly trained. Contraception and obstetrical care were years in the future. Infant mortality was high. Sanitary conditions were poor, and the contagious diseases of childhood, which modern medical science has all but wiped out, took their toll.

A walk through the burial grounds of the early and mid-1800s tells the story. This is particularly true in the yard of Bethel Methodist Church, still standing a few miles outside Lake City. The church was built with slave labor by my great-grandfather Parks. There are so many children's graves. There, side by side, I saw the graves of a man and his wife. Facing them across a narrow pathway lay the graves of their seven children, the little headstones with their names and ages looking toward their parents. The dates are all in the late 1860s and early 1870s. The oldest child was a girl who had lived for only ten years. The marker for the youngest bore no name but read simply, "Baby born," with the date and "died the same day." The other five had died in infancy or early childhood. How did their parents stand the pain?

What I know of my mother's girlhood comes largely from her sister, my much loved aunt Ouida. My mother, the most reticent of women, did not encourage intimacy. I think the endless struggle to provide the necessities of life for herself and her two children left little strength for emotional involvements. She was ambitious for us, saw to it that we lived in a good neighborhood, and worked hard to come up with the tuition for private schools. She neither invited nor gave confidences. The only bit of "sex education" I ever got from her came in the years of her marriage to my stepfather. His pathological jealousy resulted in making her almost a prisoner in her own home. He discouraged any entertaining. Even Aunt Ouida made her sisterly visits during his office hours. It was a dull life for Mother. Once she said to me, I think when I was sixteen or seventeen, "Lylah Murray, better you marry a man that beats you than one that bores you." Well, I've never been beaten, and, for sure, life with Red Barber has not been boring. The only person I ever saw Mother let down her guard with was my daughter Sarah. They enjoyed each other's company.

It was Aunt Ouida who told me of my father's courtship of Mother. She told me that when he came calling he was accompanied by a little black boy whose task it was to carry an umbrella, in case it rained, and a basket. In the basket would be the offering of the day—maybe flowers, sometimes candy, cookies baked by his mother, a great cook, and now and then a book of poems. She also told me that from the time he first saw Mother he could not have told you the color of the eyes and hair of another woman.

It was also Aunt Ouida who told me about "Aunt Aggie" and her boneyard garden. Aunt Aggie lived in a little cabin nearby. She had been one of the Parks' slaves and had stayed behind when the others left. By the time the sisters came along she was quite old and could do no work, but she was a good nurse and storyteller. The two girls spent much time with her at the cabin hearing tales of "them days." Aunt Aggie also practiced voodoo and could "cast spells." Aunt Ouida told me often about how she and my mother would slip out after the house was asleep and creep to the cabin, peep in the window, and watch the goings-on thrown into scary relief by the firelight on the hearth. Aunt Aggie also had a "boneyard garden." I think I saw it when I was very young, but maybe I was only told about it. I suppose the bones came from the family table—chicken, fish, quail, and the like with perhaps a cow's jawbone or thigh. Finger and toe bones were held to be very effective. All had certainly been used by Aunt Aggie in her voodoo practice, along with perhaps some hair from the intended victim, their purpose to remind her clientele of her dark powers which they did not doubt.

I was amazed when a Northern friend of mine said, as I spoke of Aunt Aggie, "I don't know what you are talking about. What in the world is a boneyard garden?" I had spent my formative years in an environment where the two cultures, black and white, lived side by side. There had always been black nurses and cooks, and I had grown up playing with their children. I still remember Bertha Jordan, who was mulatto and strikingly pretty. One afternoon, as a special treat, she took my brother and me to her house to play with her children. There were refreshments, cookies, and a punch which we drank from tall cranberry-red goblets, much more beautiful and exciting than anything we had at home.

There was an "inside the house" toilet, most unusual in a Negro home of that day. On the back porch was a hand pump connected I suppose to a well in the yard. We were allowed to pump our own glasses of water. The water was icy cold and so good on a hot summer afternoon. Everything in the house seemed to my brother and me exciting and very special. I have often thought what a story there must have been to be told about Bertha Jordan. Someone certainly cared enough to see that things were made a little better than was customary at that time, for her and her children.

Back to Aunt Aggie and my friend who didn't know what a

boneyard garden was. I had always known of voodoo and been fascinated by it. It was the religion of the blacks of the west coast of
Africa, particularly of Dahomey and Ghana (later, under the British,
called the Gold Coast). This was the area of the slave trade to the
Caribbean, especially Haiti, and to Brazil in South America.

The slaves came to the southern states of North America, and with
them they brought their own tribal religions. Then a strange thing
happened. They also embraced the white man's God. They accepted
the Christian ritual, the prayers, the hymns, even the saint's names
which they bestowed upon their African spirits. The hymns of my
Methodist preacher ancestors became their beautiful, moving spir-
ituals. The River Jordan became the Ohio River and Beulah Land
the states across it where there was Freedom. "Climbing Jacob's
Ladder" was the long hard flight to freedom. To me nothing tells the
Easter story more simply and beautifully than "Were you there when
they crucified my Lord?"

In the late 1960s when my husband and I were living on Key
Biscayne in Miami we saw much evidence of the melding of the two
religions. This was shortly after the period of the large influx of upper middle-class Cubans fleeing oppression under Castro. They were
people of wealth and education and had in great part been raised by
black nurses and servants.

During that time I was fortunate enough to take a course in
anthropology under a very fine professor from the University of
Miami. To one class she brought a young Cuban girl, a medical student at the university, who gave a lecture on the various cults, African in origin, operating among the Cuban exiles. She told of going
into her mother's closet and finding, carefully hidden on the top
shelf, a voodoo charm.

When she confronted her mother with the evidence she asked,
"How can you go to Mass on Sunday and do that?" Her mother only
smiled and said, "Certain things require certain cures."

". . . OF CHILDREN . . ."

As soon after my father's death as Mother was able to make arrangements with Dannie for her two children's care, she went job hunting. She had taken a business course in her short time in college, and she became secretary to a wonderful man. "Daddy Fagg," as he was called, was president of the Children's Home Society. The Home was housed in one of the large old residences on Riverside Avenue, then one of the finest residential streets in Jacksonville. There must have been about thirty children living there. It was Daddy Fagg who named it a "home"—rather than an "orphanage," the common name at that time for such a place. By hard work he was also successful in having the word "illegitimate" taken off birth certificates. He was a true pioneer in the field of child care.

My brother Mat and I were sometimes taken to the Home on Sunday afternoons for ice cream with the children, and we considered that quite a treat. One Christmas we were invited to see their tree. After our own modest Christmas morning, which must have strained my mother's resources considerably, their tree seemed enormous . . . and, oh my, the presents—boxes and boxes. With the unconscious cruelty of childhood I asked my mother why they had so many presents and we had so few.

There was another Christmas when my brother and I were a little older that was pure magic. My dear aunt Ouida had married a man with two children, Frances and Albert, who were a bit older than we were. They lived in a house in the country on the banks of the St. John's River, and we three, our mother and the two of us, were invited to spend the holiday with them. The strange house, the new cousins, their jolly father, the air of expectation, and the Christmas Eve supper at the big dining-room table all were a great treat to our little quiet family. There was much guessing about what Santa Claus would bring us. Would he really come? Could he find us in the strange house? And had we been good children? Finally we were all settled in our beds with the warning that Santa would not come until *everyone* was fast asleep. I tried and tried, but I was much too excited for sleep to come. Finally, very quietly, I crept to the window and looked out. The moon shone brightly on the clearing near the house and the woods beyond. Suddenly, at the edge of the woods there was a figure of someone pulling something behind him. Could that be Santa Claus, and if he saw me and knew I was awake would he go away? (Of course it was Aunt Ouida's husband bringing the trees he had cut, but that was not what the excited child at the window was envisioning.) I rushed back to bed and closed my eyes tight!

The morning finally came and we four children were awakened, bundled in our sweaters, and escorted downstairs. The doors to the dining room were closed. When everyone was ready in the hall the doors were thrown open, and—wonder of wonders—there in the large bay window stood *four* Christmas trees, one for each child! My *very own* tree with *my* presents under it and its candles shining! This was long before the days of electric tree lights, and after a short time for admiration of the bright candles they were carefully snuffed out and the presents were opened. I often think how anxiously the adults must have watched until the candles were safely out; a wooden pail, filled with sand, was kept at hand, just in case. Christmas dinner was in the full tradition of the Deep South. There was the mammoth turkey, as well as ham, string beans, candied sweet potatoes and boiled onions, and, for dessert, ambrosia made with oranges, bananas, apples, freshly grated coconut, and red cherries. With the ambrosia there was a choice of four cakes: Lady Baltimore with its rich nut-and-raisin filling, a white cake with lemon filling and coconut icing, a many-layered chocolate one, and, in the tradition, fruit cake.

After the gargantuan feast the children were turned loose in the living room to play with our new toys. I wish I could report that the euphoria of the day continued; but, alas, my brother Mat and I ended up in a hair-pulling fight, over some toy, I presume. The next thing I knew there was Mother standing in the door and I was threatened with banishment should any more disturbance be heard.

Of the seven years I lived in my stepfather's house I do not recall a single Christmas. Of course there had to have been celebrations of a sort, but the memories of them are gone. It is just as well. The prayer book says it: "The burden of them is intolerable."

Aunt Ouida and Mr. Hitey, as her husband was called by us, became a large part of the treats of our childhood. He was a physician and what the nickname came from I never knew. After the big house on the St. John's River they lived in a series of small towns in South Georgia and Central Florida. He seems to have been a sort of itinerant doctor who would go where there was a need of medical care.

Mr. Hitey was an outdoors person and a hunter, and I was often invited to share outings. I remember canoe trips down beautiful small rivers in Central Florida. One river was a sort of milky jade in color and very beautiful. I have described it to a number of people, but no one has been able to place it for me. Sometimes I think I might have dreamed it out of one of the beautifully illustrated fairytale books that I had been given. Be that as it may, he taught me how to paddle a canoe and enjoy the quiet mystery of those wild rivers.

I also went hunting with him, and he taught me to stay behind the hunter and always to look before I put my foot down in those sandy woods, lest I trespass on the territory of a rattlesnake. We would return from the hunt, sometimes with quail and other times with rabbit. Aunt Ouida would always have a pot of grits ready and we would have a feast.

About that time I was also introduced to the pleasures of avocados (alligator pears, they were called then, I suppose because of their tough, dark skins) and mangoes—no hybrids, they were just the small, fibrous, juicy native fruit. We children had two choices, either to eat them over the kitchen sink or to go outdoors with them. There were also guavas, but I became acquainted with them later when I would visit Aunt Fanny who lived in Fort Pierce. These were all rather exotic tastes for a young child, but not for anything would I have admitted I found them strange and thus have lost caste. Of course I soon learned to delight in them all.

Aunt Ouida, with automobile and dog.

Aunt Ouida and Mr. Hitey were always doing exciting things. Theirs was the first automobile I remember, and in the summer there were trips to Atlantic Beach on the ocean. These were all-day excursions, which often included a tire change along the way. The road was a narrow brick one, and meeting another car headed in the other direction was always an adventure undertaken with great caution. Preparation for the trip itself was elaborate. There was lunch to be prepared and bathing suits and towels to be packed. The order of events on arrival at the beach began with a change into suits. This took place inside the automobile, with rain curtains put up for a suggestion of privacy. Then a nice long swim was followed by the picnic lunch. After eating we rested, most reluctantly, but on strict orders from the doctor. Then back into the water we went for a second swim before dressing for the long ride to Jacksonville. Now the same trip takes an easy half-hour on a four-lane highway.

Years later when the stepchildren were grown, Aunt Ouida and

Mr. Hitey were divorced, but they always remained friends. When she lay dying in the hospital following a gall-bladder operation (the wound became infected), he came to visit her. So did Frances, the stepdaughter, with her daughter, Frances Ouida. I think anyone who ever knew Aunt Ouida loved her. During that long illness, when several blood transfusions were needed there was never a paid donor. She had worked for years as nurse-receptionist in a doctor's office, and patients as well as personal friends came to give blood.

Aunt Ouida was so wise, except about picking husbands. She had three divorces. But even about that she was philosophical. When a relative who was in the process of a second divorce said, "But Ouida, I thought this one was different," she replied, "All men are different, but all husbands are the same."

AUNT MOLLIE

Most of the early settlers of North Florida came from Georgia and the Carolinas. They were largely English stock and farmers and planters by livelihood. However, there were also followers of John and Charles Wesley, hardy Methodist preachers who pushed from Savannah into the hills of North Georgia to bring the Gospel to the heathen, by no means all of whom were Indians.

My maternal grandfather Watts was the son of a circuit rider, as the Methodist preachers were called. I was told as a child how the rider, when he went into a new town, would often be challenged by the town bully and forced to establish his authority in personal combat. I am proud of my great-grandfather Watts, who rode the circuit, and of his resolute, uncomplaining wife who shared the hard life with him.

There was a summer vacation I spent with Great-Aunt Mollie in Boston, Georgia. She was the daughter of the preacher who rode the circuit in the clay hills of North Georgia. Her brother, my grandfather Watts, was Dannie's husband. Boston, just across the state line from Monticello, Florida, was actually a village of dirt roads. There was a Methodist church, a library, and a grocery store. Aunt Mollie's house sat on a large piece of ground just across from the library. By then I had discovered the joy and the escape of reading. Every weekday morning I would walk over to the library and carefully make my selection for the day's reading, returning the book that I had devoured the day before. I must have read all the *Bobbsey Twins* and all the *Fairy Tales—Blue, Yellow, Green*, etc. These beautifully illustrated books contained many of the Andersen and Grimm stories.

Aunt Mollie's daughter, Cousin Eula, who would have been seventeen or eighteen at the time, was always kind. She taught me how to swim in the town pool. The water was very cold; I imagine it was spring-fed.

There were other ways Cousin Eula made my summer pleasant. There was a peach orchard nearby where the townspeople, for a small fee, could pick their own fruit. Picking peaches was a social occasion. She and her young friends would take me with them. There was chatter and laughter. She and I would also go to neighbors' gardens to pick the vegetables for the family table. Aunt Mollie was an excellent cook, and it was from her that I learned to eat tripe. I enjoyed it and was dismayed a few years later when I learned it was the cow's stomach.

There was a piano in the house. Cousin Eula had a pleasing voice, and in the evenings she and her friends would gather and sing the songs of the day. I particularly remember her singing "Poor Butterfly." In later years I lived in New York as a grown woman and often heard Puccini's *Butterfly* at the Metropolitan, and I never failed to think of Cousin Eula.

Until that summer in Boston, Georgia, all my church experience had been Episcopal. My father's people (they had been Tories in the Carolinas during the Revolution) were Church of England and later, of course, Episcopalian. But in Aunt Mollie's house everybody went to the Methodist church for Sunday morning service and Wednesday evening Prayer Meeting. On Sunday evenings there was hymn singing at church, and I loved it. The warmth and enthusiasm and the words—oh those wonderful words, each hymn a story. "Throw out the life line—there is a brother none other can save" (what a challenge!), and

> I come to the garden alone
> While the dew is still on the roses;
> And the voice I hear falling on my ear
> The Son of God discloses.
>
> He speaks and the sound of his voice
> Is so sweet the birds hush their singing
> And the melody that He gave to me
> Within my heart is ringing—
>
> And He walks with me, and He talks with me,
> And He tells me I am his own,

And the joy we share as we tarry there,
None other has ever known.

Aunt Mollie told me stories of her father and the circuit riding days, and how she grew up moving from one parsonage to another, as her father was transferred every two years. What hardy people those men were and what fortitude their women had. Aunt Mollie's mother—she would have been my great-grandmother—had grown up on a plantation, and her father was shocked when she was determined to marry the itinerant preacher and embrace that hard life. At least she must take her personal servant with her. The preacher, of course, was opposed to slavery and insisted that she be freed. She was, but no one ever told her. She was a fine seamstress and children's nurse and what a lifesaver she must have been to the young wife. She lived out her days a beloved member of the family.

After Cousin Eula was married she and her husband, Cousin Judson Bibb, came to Jacksonville to live and Aunt Mollie also came to spend her last years with them.

When Red and I decided to marry I took him to Cousin Eula's house to meet some of my family. By that time Aunt Mollie was quite elderly, but there she sat in her special armchair surrounded by her daughters, Eula, Pauline, and Lila (the family name again but with a slightly different spelling). She wore a black skirt and a white shirtwaist with a high stiff collar. Around her collar was a black velvet ribbon held at her chin with a Victorian cameo pin. Her hair was twisted into a bun and held in place with tortoise-shell combs. Except for the natural changes of age, she must have looked much as she did as a young wife.

Cousins Pauline and Lila, Aunt Mollie's other two daughters, were by then both widows and lived much of the time with their younger sister. About that recurring family name, mine is spelled Lylah, Cousin Eula's daughter and granddaughter are Lilas. I am told the name was an inheritance from those Methodist preacher ancestors who were great scholars of the Bible and comes from a Hebrew word meaning "dark night." I am sure my young husband-to-be must have looked at that room full of women and wondered, "Where are the men?" He has since implied as much.

Cousin Eula was a tall, handsome woman with long straight hair. Her eyes and hair were very black. She had a great sense of style and loved pretty clothes and shoes. Her vocabulary was filled with rich earthy sayings which she had heard as a child in Boston. Two I particularly remember were, "If your burden gits too heavy, lay hit down," and "Do a little plowing every day. If you stop, you're a goner."

The last time I saw Cousin Eula was when I flew to Jacksonville to attend the fiftieth anniversary of the founding of the School of Nursing at Riverside Hospital. I stayed with Sarah Spears who had been a pioneer in the field of nurse education and was a dear friend for whom I had named my daughter. Cousin Eula and Judson came by and took me to the airport to catch the plane for my flight home. The dark hair was snow-white and for the only time I heard her speak of age. "I'm old now," she said, "and don't go out much anymore."

Three weeks later I was back in Jacksonville for her funeral. As is the custom in the Methodist Church, at her funeral her preacher spoke of her long years of service to her church, of her kind and loving nature. He said, "Sister Eula was not in church Sunday morning so I went calling on her in the afternoon. She told me, 'I am ready.'"

Before the week was out she had gone. "If your burden gits too heavy, lay hit down."

After Cousin Eula's death Judson remarried. Estelle was younger and was a devoted member of the Methodist church which all three of them attended. It was a happy marriage, and she was kind and supportive as he aged. He died quietly in his sleep in his own bed, in the house where he and Cousin Eula had raised their children and he and Estelle had continued to live. He was ninety-four. I flew from our home in Tallahassee to be present at the funeral service. By the time I arrived the house was filled. Everyone was related either by blood or marriage. His two sons were there with their wives and sons. His daughter, Mary Lila, had died, but his granddaughter, Lila, came and brought her nine-month-old son Ronald, Judson's great-grandson.

I was the oldest person there. I realized with a mixture of shock and pride that now I am the matriarch of the tribe.

THE DARK DAYS

When I was quite young, about eight years old, I became a boarding student at the Diocesan School for Girls in Gainesville, Florida. The school had been founded in 1873, but its association with the Episcopal Diocese of Florida was new. It received its diocesan endorsement in 1906, and I was a student there in 1914. The school's founders were Miss Margaret Tebeau, of Staunton, Virginia, and Mrs. Sarah Caroline Messison Thomas, probably from the same city. By the time I was there Mrs. Thomas had died and her daughter Alice had taken her place. Miss Alice was then fifty-three years old. Miss Maggie was an incredible seventy-nine, but still very much in command. The school was the first of its kind for girls in Central Florida.

After Miss Maggie's death in 1924, Miss Alice continued to supervise the school until ill health forced her to retire in 1936. By the terms of Miss Maggie's will the school became the property of the diocese in 1934. A few days after Miss Alice's death in 1948 the diocese sold the property to the city of Gainesville, which allowed the nursery school to continue to operate until 1951. Seventy-eight years after its founding, Miss Maggie's was no more. The charming old house which sat in its beautiful garden filled with camellias (called japonicas then) and azaleas is gone, the tennis court and the playground with its swings have been bulldozed, and the entire block is now a city metered parking lot. The Sunday afternoon I saw it again many years later, the meters all read "Time Elapsed."

Both Miss Maggie and Miss Alice were "maiden ladies." Miss Maggie had been a young woman during the Civil War, and Miss Alice had been born the year the war began. Schoolgirl gossip had it that Miss Maggie's lover had been killed in the fighting during the war, and that a later attempt at elopement by Miss Alice had been discovered and thwarted.

Miss Maggie, who was headmistress, was a tiny bird-like lady with white hair which she wore in bangs at her forehead and temples. It was held in a bun on top of her head with an elegant tortoise-shell comb. She had an aura of authority, and when she sat at her desk on a raised platform, she became positively regal. We all respected and feared her, though I cannot recall her voice ever being raised or, for that matter, any discipline being meted out by her.

Miss Alice was another matter. She was younger, a large, dark-haired woman who always seemed to be dressed in plain, drab clothing. Her overall appearance was unattractive and somehow managed to convey the impression of a "poor relation." What a contrast she was to Miss Maggie, whose pretty clothes seemed, even to a child, to speak of style and taste. Miss Alice had a temper, a strident voice, and she could be *mean*. She did some teaching and also seemed to be responsible for all housekeeping arrangements. Besides these two there was a younger woman—and sometimes still another—who did most of the basic teaching.

Miss Maggie taught piano. For what reason I do not know, for I certainly had no talent, I was one of her pupils. Perhaps it was just one of the pleasing skills taught to any properly educated young girl of the times. Anyway, struggle with the keyboard she and I did, with the help of a wooden pointer with which she pointed to the written notes and cracked my knuckles, by way of emphasis, when I played the wrong ones. Along with the exercise book there was also a book of songs which I loved. It contained such tidbits as "La Paloma" and "Juanita" and "Marching Through Georgia." Miss Maggie took one look at "Marching," promptly fetched needle and thread, and sewed together the pages of the hated Yankee song commemorating Sherman's march from Atlanta to the sea.

Despite my lack of musical talent, not all was loss. I had a quick mind, a retentive memory, and a feeling for the cadence and beauty of the written and the spoken word. Every Friday afternoon before school recessed for the weekend was given over to the recitation of poetry, and there I shone! There were Edgar Allan Poe's "Annabelle Lee" and "The Bells" and a wonderful poem about an Indian maiden who loved a cowboy. I still remember "and she sat on forlorn

Margaret Tebeau's school, Gainesville.

while the man-child was born." How I yearned to know just what
that meant; what was she sitting on, and why?

I must have been no more than eight years old when my mother
took me to be a boarder at Miss Maggie's. I remember sitting with
Mother in a parlor filled with lovely Victorian furniture. Its formal
elegance was apparent even to the small child. I never saw that room
again; I associate it only with my first day at boarding school. I can't
remember any emotion connected with the parting from my mother.
Surely it must have cost the young widow pain to leave behind her
small child. Or was she so overwhelmed by the loss of her husband,
by the lack of financial security, and by the realization of her responsibility to provide for the needs of two small children that she was
numb? I choose to think so.

Anyway, Mother left, and I was taken upstairs to a small bedroom
at the end of a hall and told that it was to be my room. I have often
wondered where the money for my tuition came from; maybe from

Miss Maggie, owner and headmistress.

Uncle Fred? At any rate, I was soon made to understand that I was not there on quite the same terms as the other boarders. My first reaction that evening was to a sense of darkness. Indeed, I suppose if I were asked to describe my days at Miss Maggie's in one word, I would have to say *Dark*. Even today, all the good times, and there have been so many in my later years, have not entirely erased the bitterness. However, the harsh discipline did challenge the quick mind, and awakened in me the determination to be the smartest, to make the highest grades, to be special. Instead of destroying me it strengthened the iron in me and fortified my will to survive. On the other hand, my brother, who was there for a short time a year later, was crushed by the same experience and retreated into his own private world, from which he was never to emerge quite completely.

The boarders usually numbered about ten to fifteen pupils and except for the short time Mat was there, so far as I know, consisted only of girls. The day students, however, included both boys and girls. Students were classified into primary, intermediate, and senior groups. Each division covered four years of instruction but apparently each student advanced, more or less, at his own speed. When I left the school and became a day student at St. Joseph's Academy in Jacksonville, placing me was quite a challenge for the nuns.

Our school days at Miss Maggie's followed a set routine. For the boarders there was an early rising bell, and a quick dressing, followed by morning prayer (in the winter, long before the dawn broke) in the big classroom. The order of prayer came from the "Forms of Prayer to be Used in Families" in the Book of Common Prayer. The prayers always seemed so long to me in the cold and the dark. Recently I looked them up in the little leather *Prayer Book and Hymnal* with my name on the front in gold letters (the 1790 version, which was the first to be used in the Episcopal Church in America) that my mother gave me when I was eight years old. I was surprised at how short the prayers really are. But there were the old memories: "accept this our morning sacrifice of praise and thanksgiving for His sake who lay down in the grave," and "keep in our minds a lively remembrance of that great day, in which we must give a strict account of our thoughts, words and actions . . . be eternally rewarded or punished . . . by the Judge of the quick and the dead."

Our school day finished with Evening Prayer. "Defend us from all dangers and mischiefs and from the fear of them"; "make us ever mindful of the time when we shall lie down in the dust"; and, "grant us grace always to live in such a state that we may never be afraid to die, so that living and dying we may be Thine." Pretty strong words for an eight-year-old, but not a bad guidepost for living, and I've never been afraid of dying.

Following prayers, the typical day at Miss Maggie's began with a short exercise period on the tennis court, and then breakfast, including the saying of Grace, of course. After breakfast we went upstairs, made our beds, brushed our teeth with charcoal, and combed our hair. We were then ready for the arrival of those fortunates, the day students, and classes. Roll was called, and each child answered with his or her own memorized response from the Bible or the Book of Common Prayer. Since the students were of different ages and varying grades, everyone had a different gem to offer in response to the calling of his or her name; it was much more interesting than a muttered "Present." Miss Maggie always called the roll.

To the best of my recollection we began with the Catechism, and when that was perfected we continued with certain prayers that were deemed appropriate. To this day I remember them word for word. Somewhere along the way we progressed to the Bible, beginning with Genesis, verse by verse. There I discovered the "begats," the "lay withs," and the "he knew his wife"—nothing as explicit as the instruction children receive today, but mighty exciting and perplexing, and certainly carrying the connotation of the taboo. Needless to say, no explanation was offered.

After classes were finished there was a period of games and other play. I remember being introduced to tennis, rope skipping, and croquet. Give a couple of aggressive eight-, nine-, or ten-year-olds mallets and wooden balls, and that can be worked into considerable excitement. Study hall followed, then supper, evening prayers, and so to bed.

Saturday's routine was of course different. There were beds to be
made with fresh linen, hair to be shampooed, and the week's personal laundry to be collected and a list to be made. I don't know who
did the girls' personal laundry, but I do remember being allowed to
take Miss Maggie's stiff collars, which she wore with her shirtwaist,
across the street to the Chinese laundry. The owner, and sole worker
as far as I knew, would give me litchi nuts. He became one of the
special friends of my childhood. I was wise enough not to tell anyone
of the treat.

Then there was a sewing class. I learned to make clothes for my
baby doll, whom I had named Edgar Allan Poe, and to darn stockings. I hated those ugly black stockings and the tedious darning.
Having made my escape, I have refused to this day to mend hose;
one run, and out they go. My poor brother—I remember once while
he was at Miss Maggie's school with me he was swinging so enthusi-
astically in the playground swing that he went too high and was
thrown to the ground. As he lay there, I ran to him crying, with
sisterly concern, "Did you tear your stockings?" It was my duty to
keep his clothes in order. How lonely the little boy must have been,
the only one of his sex, with all of us females.

At a set date in the fall our long winter underwear was gotten out
of the trunk and was then worn until the appointed day in spring, no
matter what the temperature. I must confess that when the hot
weather came I would take the underwear, which I had not worn the
preceding week, wipe the floor under my bed with it to make it
appear well worn, and add it to my soiled week's laundry. So early
does necessity teach us deception. How I struggled to tuck the long
white cotton legs of that hated underwear inside the black ribbed
stockings.

After the Saturday noonday meal everyone wrote a letter home to
parents; no idle hands for the Devil's workshop at Miss Maggie's.
Sometimes when the weather was good we were taken in line two by
two for a walk in town, and that was exciting. Of course there were
some special treats. I remember going to the courthouse square for

the Confederate Memorial Day observance and enjoying the lovely flowers, the flags, the speeches, and a parade. In those years there were numerous veterans of the Civil War still living. Many of them were the grandfathers of my classmates, but they marched along quite spryly and pretty young girls gave them flowers.

Sundays at Miss Maggie's began with early Communion at the church for the older girls. We little ones who had not yet been confirmed did not go, and that meant a late sleep, which was a treat. Of course everyone went to the eleven o'clock service. We sat together, with Miss Alice in command in the first pew and Miss Maggie in the back, her eyes trained on all of us. After church and while waiting for Sunday dinner we memorized the Collect for the day, which was sometimes varied with a hymn. Both I loved; the beautiful poetry was so easy to learn. I don't remember much about Sunday afternoon. I'm sure it was spent in a respectful, appropriate way. I do recall one of the older girls reading stories aloud to the group, and that was nice.

Occasionally my godmother, Mrs. Birkett Jordan, would take me home with her from church service for Sunday dinner. Her daughter and son, Esther and Birkett, and I would play together, and I loved the freedom. Many townspeople were kind to me in those years. The ties between Holy Trinity Church parishioners and the school were close. Most of their children were day students there.

One example of their kindness I still remember most vividly. I became ill, and a throat culture revealed that I had diphtheria. I was isolated in a bedroom on the third floor of the house with a nurse, a pretty young woman with blonde curly hair. She was on duty twenty-four hours a day for the whole time of my illness. Except for the first few days, when I was quite ill and ran a high fever, I was comfortable, and it was largely a matter of waiting until I produced a negative throat culture. The nurse was most kind; she read to me a great deal, and we played endless games. My schoolwork was sent up daily, and she helped me keep abreast. The townsfolk sent me many presents, mostly games and books and needlework. Miss Nora

Norton had a gift shop and was particularly generous. When I returned to Gainesville as a bride I was surprised and delighted to see that the shop was still functioning and filled with lovely gifts.

I must now write about the *Rites of Spring* according to Miss Maggie. I don't know that all boarders received the same treatment, but this is how it went for me. On the selected pre-spring Friday afternoon, about suppertime, a series of calomel pills was given to me at regular intervals; perhaps every hour, I'm not sure. However, I do remember vividly the horrible griping stomach pains and the nausea that followed. I was put to bed, without supper, needless to say. After a miserable night the ritual was resumed, while it was still dark, with a cupful of warm castor oil followed by an orange to suck, supposedly to take away the taste of the oil. I was then considered clean and ready to face spring.

It took hours of analysis and many of my husband's dollars to exorcise that particular ghost, and to convince me that I did not have to punish myself with nausea and vomiting for what hidden sins I did not know. Only recently I discovered a fellow pilgrim, a young friend whose parents, Air Force personnel, spent several years in England while she was a young girl. There she attended an English boarding school, and there also castor oil (minus the calomel) was given as a punishment. Oh, those Victorian ancestors! They are with us yet. It interests me that recently when I spoke to my young doctor of the calomel, his reply was, "Calomel, what's that?" His response was heartening. Some progress has been made over the years.

Miss Alice's discipline was always harsh, and to a young child often impossible to understand. I remember the fall when Mother was preparing my wardrobe for the return to school. I had outgrown my winter coat and Mother took me shopping for a new one. My choice was a happy, bright blue with a black and white velvet collar. Both of us were delighted with it. But my pride was short-lived. Miss Alice supervised the unpacking of my trunk. When the coat was discovered, her response was immediate: "This is entirely unsuitable." The coat and I were taken to Wilson's Dry Goods Store that very afternoon, and my beautiful coat was exchanged for an ugly, drab, cheap one. How surprised Mother must have been when I returned to Jacksonville for the Christmas holiday. I still wonder how many lunches Mother skipped to make possible the purchase of the pretty coat.

During the early 1900s in small Southern towns such as Gainesville, parades provided much of the community entertainment. Motion pictures, radio, and television were in the distant future. Miss Maggie's school faced the town's main street, and boarding students were allowed to stand on the sidewalk to watch the parades go by. I remember one in particular. My godmother had just purchased a brand-new, shiny Model-T Ford, one of the first in town. She invited me to ride in it with Esther and Birkett, as part of one of the parades. I was ecstatic. Miss Alice said, however, "No, . . . it would make you different from the other boarders." I fought back the tears as I stood on the sidewalk and watched my friends ride by. Their happy waves to me were no consolation.

Another forlorn memory, this one with a somewhat happy ending, remains vivid after all the long years. Commencement and the end of the school year were a time of great excitement. There was the school play, the awarding of prizes for the highest average in each of the three departments, and much reciting of poems. The tie of the school to the Episcopal diocese was accentuated when Bishop Weed came down from Jacksonville to preside at the festivities. He was then quite elderly, and such a dear. In his Episcopal robes he radiated gentle friendliness, and all of us children loved him. Most of the older ones had been confirmed by him, and he was also the person who gave out the coveted prizes.

A few weeks before commencement, when school opened one morning it was discovered that someone had taken toilet paper and decorated the playground and garden most extensively. For some reason Miss Alice elected to lay the blame on me. My protests were of no avail, my pleas of innocence unheeded. I was meted out a large number of demerits and punished. The injustice was all the greater because the act was so against my nature. I have always hated vulgarity, and to this day cringe at the telling of "dirty jokes."

Now to commencement and the awarding of prizes. A girl was called to receive the gold cross and chain for the highest average in the primary department, of which I was also a student. Then my name was called and I went forward to Miss Maggie's desk where Bishop Weed was sitting. He handed me a small box and began to read aloud the accompanying card that said I actually had the highest average but because I had a large number of demerits I was being given the empty box that had held the cross and chain. I remember so well the look of shock on his face. Then he said, in a loud voice that still sounds in my heart, "Don't you worry, I would rather be smart than good." How I loved him.

Later that afternoon he went back to Jacksonville on the train and took me with him, to be delivered at the station to my mother. We ate ice cream in the parlor car and had a wonderful time. I think he told my mother what had happened, because when my birthday came a month later there was my gold cross and chain from her.

I was never again at Miss Maggie's.

AND THERE WAS LIGHT . . .

When I was fifteen my mother remarried. I didn't know of the marriage until it was an accomplished fact. We knew that the man for whom she was secretary and office manager often brought her home from work, but we had not met him. There was a hanging swing on the front screened porch, and they sometimes sat there in the dark on summer evenings and talked. Their voices were low and we could not distinguish the words. My brother Mat, to whom he had occasionally sent science fiction magazines, frustrated by being unable to understand the words of their conversation, finally said to me, "Buzz, buzz, that's all I hear. I'm going to call him Mr. Buzz." The name stuck. I think it sort of pleased him when he became our stepfather. Perhaps it indicated a kind of acceptance.

It was at this time that I became, for a short while, a boarder at St. Joseph's Academy in St. Augustine. I suppose I wondered why the change was necessary, but it was essentially the same environment in which I felt so secure at St. Joseph's in Jacksonville, and I accepted it. The reason was soon made clear. Mother came from Jacksonville to see me, and it was then she told me that she and Mr. Thomas had driven to Savannah, where they had been married and where they spent a few days. I would be coming to Jacksonville at Christmas, she said; Mat and I would be living with them in a house of our own, near where Dannie lived.

She had come down in a chauffeur-driven automobile and brought with her a big box of fried chicken for me to share with my friends. My first reaction was one of excitement and pleasant surprise. Like my friends, now I would have a home with a father in it. Since my father's death when I was five I had lived in a completely matriarchal household. That Mother had not told me about it beforehand did not seem strange to me. She had never shared any of her feelings, happy or otherwise, with me. Now she would be home all day and we would have a chance to get to know each other.

That was not exactly how it worked out. It was a new role for all of us—stepfather, stepchildren, wife—after years of solitary independence, with leisure hours to be filled. The tension was soon obvious. It was hardest for my brother Mat—and for my stepfather, I suppose. They were foreordained to be contestants for my mother's attention, and my stepfather held all the cards.

It must have been quite a bold decision for the granddaughter of the Methodist preacher to place her child in a Catholic school like St. Joseph's Academy. How glad I am she did, for my days at the two academies with the nuns were very different from my time at Miss Maggie's. Both in Jacksonville, where I was a day student, and twice in St. Augustine, where I boarded, I was very happy.

The academy in Jacksonville, where I had my first contact with the sisters, was clear across town. When I first began as a student there I made the long streetcar ride, about an hour I believe it was, daily. However, the ride did give me time to do some of my homework. Sister St. Andrew, the grammarian, piled it on. She didn't spend too much time on math, but she was tough on dangling participles and such.

From the seventh through twelfth grades, I only had one poor teacher at the academies. She was a timid little young nun who tried for a short time to teach us Latin. We were merciless; she could not keep us under control, though she tried so hard. She was soon replaced, and I've often wondered what became of her—shifted I suppose to a non-teaching niche in the system.

After my mother and Mr. Thomas, my stepfather, were married I rode to school in the family automobile. It was driven by Henry, who doubled as our yardman and heavy house cleaner. We dropped my stepfather at his office, and Henry then took me on to school. However, I made him let me out a block away, for I didn't want my friends to see me arriving chauffeur-driven. The academy was in a middle-class neighborhood, and the people were genteel and kind; but most of them didn't have cars, much less chauffeurs.

My schooldays were long because of the commuting. There was just time when I returned home in the late afternoon to wash up for dinner, and do my homework after the evening meal. Since I did not go to the school near our house, I had no friends in the neighborhood. All my friends were the five-day students at the academy. Weekends were lonely, and my time was spent with books.

My stepfather was ill-suited for companionship with teenagers and pathologically jealous of Mother and the time and attention she gave to my brother and me. Mat and I spent much of the adolescent years, after Mother's remarriage, on a shuttle between home and boarding school. Most of the time I was at home; but Mat was more often away at school. Partly because we were seldom home at the same time, we became almost strangers; we were both grown up and married before we became brother and sister again.

Mr. Thomas owned an advertising agency, and one of his clients was Riverside Military Academy. Mat spent some time there on a "due bill." There was another school somewhere in North Georgia, not a very good one, and in his senior year Mat ran away. Not until the Second World War, while in the Army Air Corps, did he complete the requirements for his high school diploma. After serving overseas he returned to civilian life, and was a frequent student at the Massey Business College, finally achieving a degree in business administration.

The two nuns I remember so well in my high school years were Sister Theresa Joseph and Sister Constance. Sister Theresa Joseph was tall, almost regal, and quite handsome with large, soft brown eyes—in her early forties I would guess. She was school principal, and taught history, chemistry, and English and American literature. Her voice was deep, almost theatrical, and she read the English poets, Shelley, Keats, Byron, even Oscar Wilde, with much love. I can still hear her, with that beautiful voice, saying, "Yet each man kills the thing he loves. . . . The coward does it with a kiss, The brave man with a sword." Or: "St. Agnes' Eve—Ah, bitter chill it was! The owl, for all his feathers, was a-cold."

Later when Red was broadcasting for CBS and we were in Miami for an Orange Bowl game, Sister Theresa Joseph was in charge of the downtown parochial school, and we had a nice visit. Another time, on our way to spring training with the Brooklyn Dodgers at Daytona Beach we drove through St. Augustine, where she was then mother superior of the order. I took our seven-year-old daughter in to meet her. I never saw her again. She died after a long illness at Mercy Hospital in Miami.

Sister Constance was younger, somewhere between thirty and thirty-five, and had snapping, black, black eyes in very white skin. She was short and slender and quick in all her movements. In her severe black habit she made a most dramatic picture. She taught mathematics, Spanish, and, for some reason, astronomy. She was an excellent teacher, very demanding, and no one ever pulled any wool over those snapping eyes. With me it was love at first sight, and she soon became part mother, part sister. I don't know how she sensed my lonely home life, but she did. She would let me stay and visit after school was out. My senior year I went back to the academy on Saturday afternoons, and she and I read Cicero together. I regret to have to report that all I remember of Cicero is that episode in which the young men danced naked on the banquet table—or was it the young women?

That last year I wanted very much to become a Catholic. Sister Constance said that nothing could make her happier, but that I would have to wait until I had been away from the convent and its influence for one year. She was wise. I am much too akin to my Methodist preacher ancestors. It would have been a mistake. Several years later, while I was in training at Riverside Hospital in Jacksonville, I would now and then go to see her and try my doubts and fears against her sounding board. Of course I took my young man to pass inspection. When we had been married several years and it looked as though we might not have a child, Sister Constance was on a pilgrimage to Lourdes. She wrote me from there that she had prayed that I might give birth to a child. I do not know what her illness was, but she died quite young. I am glad she lived to know her prayers were answered and that I had my daughter.

My time in St. Augustine as a boarder was rich, steeped in the beauty of the Catholic ritual. I was in my teens, and most responsive.

Even though I was a Protestant, I loved the mystery of the ritual of the Mass—the Latin, the flickering candlelight, the statues of St. Joseph and the Virgin at the two side altars, and the soft voices of the nuns singing the hymns, some in English, others in Latin. Our days ended, as they began, in quiet and beauty. On the dormitory floor there was a long corridor with rooms off either side. At the far end there stood a life-size statue of the Blessed Virgin. Here, teeth brushed, hair combed, and faces washed, we all knelt in our gowns and robes and recited the *Litany of the Blessed Virgin Mary* which dates back to the sixteenth century. I still remember many of the words: "Mother of good counsel," "Virgin most merciful," "Mystical rose," "Morning star," "Queen of angels," "Queen of peace," "Pray for us." How safe I felt with the Virgin watching over me through the dark of the night. I must say that I never once was proselytized, but my life has been made richer by those years with the nuns.

The nuns' clothing, their "habits," were rigidly the same, but underneath those habits dwelt a wide variety of personalities. Sister Elizabeth taught art, including china painting. She was quite old and indulgent to us girls. On the other hand, Sister Rose de Lima who was much younger, and taught Latin and Spanish, was sarcastic and demanding, but an exciting teacher and always fair. I would work very hard for praise from her. After my days in St. Augustine she moved to Jacksonville, where she became principal of the parochial school, and there our acquaintance was renewed.

Mother Marie Louise, who was in charge of all of the Sisters of St. Joseph in Florida, lived in St. Augustine in the Mother House, and we seldom saw her. If a girl were sent to her it generally meant either distressing news from home or severe discipline. I recall the time one homesick girl ran away. She was quickly found and brought back. Her parents were sent for and told she was not emotionally suited for boarding school and should be withdrawn. It was done in a most kindly fashion, and she bade us all a tearful farewell.

We did have one weekly contact with Mother Superior Marie Louise. Each Sunday, after High Mass at the cathedral, we all went to the large "study hall" and Mother read to us about etiquette! One session was taken up with table manners. I still smile when I recall the instruction for eating fresh asparagus; none of us had ever seen any. So far as we knew it was born mushy and rather tasteless in a can. Not so, according to Mother's book. One picked up a stalk very daintily with the thumb and forefinger and conveyed it to the mouth. She did her best to prepare us to take our places in "society."

The academy buildings were U-shaped. The auditorium on the ground floor and the students' sleeping quarters on the two floors above occupied one arm, the chapel and the nuns' living quarters the other, with the dining room on the ground floor, and classrooms above in the center portion. The whole complex was united on the second and third floors by wide verandahs. They were our recreation areas when it rained or when one was perhaps not well enough for more active play on the tennis and basketball courts in the area behind the buildings. These porches were Sister Elizabeth's special domain. Sometimes her art lessons took place there. The deep pockets of her habit always seemed to be filled with cookies which she shared with us. One morning, when I chose, as I often did, to go to early Mass in the chapel along with the Catholic girls, I was seated in a pew alongside Sister Elizabeth's prayer chair. She reached into her pocket, for her rosary beads I suppose, but came up by mistake with a handful of animal crackers, which scattered on the chapel floor.

Sister Annunciata, who taught one of the lower grades, fourth or fifth perhaps, had entered the novitiate along with a younger sister who later had renounced her vows, left the convent, and returned to secular life. This made Sister most interesting. We felt she was sad and missed her younger sister, whom we were sure "left for love." It was more likely that she found the discipline too severe, and her vocation not as strong as she had hoped. After classes were over for the day Sister Annunciata took charge of the outdoor recreation area. She would pin up her black habit skirt around her waist (there seemed to be numerous black petticoats underneath, just enough

Lylah, upon graduation from St. Joseph's Academy, Jacksonville. Dannie made the dress.

shorter to give some freedom of movement) and teach us tennis and referee basketball games.

I played forward on the junior team, the only athletic achievement of my school years until later when I played goalie on the hockey team at college. I was not interested in sports, and I spent the required time composing sonnets in my head. I was then planning to follow in Edna St. Vincent Millay's footsteps.

My fondness for poetry, and my natural proclivity to "show off" a bit, once got me in trouble with Sister Theresa Joseph, headmistress of the academy in Jacksonville. She also was my English teacher and had assigned a 500-word theme on October for our homework. Instead I wrote a sonnet, with which I was quite smitten. I still think it was pretty good, and it was correct in construction. Anyway, when I got my paper back it was marked *Failed*. I was shocked and asked why. Said Sister, "You didn't follow instructions." How hard it is to learn obedience.

We girls all had our favorite nuns. My favorite in St. Augustine was Sister Alberta. She taught math and history, and she was a "whiz." She had a unique way of keeping things under control. Punishment for misbehavior was sure and certain and most constructive. The offender was given a number of math problems (long division, complicated columns to add, and a history quiz or so). The work could only be done during the afternoon recreation time, and it was frustrating for the guilty one to hear the other children enjoying themselves. I remember once when I was given a particularly difficult assignment. I was determined to do it perfectly and show Sister Alberta. When I finished and handed it to her she didn't even look at it, just filed it in the wastebasket. I could have wept.

During my junior year one of my classmates, Claire Ortagus, left us and went to St. Augustine to join the novitiate. What excitement that created among us. We mulled the pros and cons endlessly.

Only three or four years ago Red and I were returning to Tallahassee, where we now live, by way of St. Augustine. We had planned to see the restored area of the Old City, but the rain was pouring, and I asked my husband to drive by the convent and just let me take a look. He stopped the car out front and said, "Why don't you go in?" I was overcome with shyness, but he insisted; so I got out of the car and ran in the rain to the front door. I rang the bell, just like the one I had rung more than fifty years before. After waiting a while just as I had long ago, a sister answered. I stammered my explanation, that I had been a boarder there so many years ago, and asked, "Could I please come in and just see the chapel?" "But of course," was the reply. I was aghast. The beautiful arched, louvered doors that ran the length of the nave on either side and opened onto a view of the garden had been closed in so that the chapel could be air-conditioned. I know that air conditioning is a great blessing in the long hot summer, as is the heat in the damp cold of January and February, for that matter. Yet the chapel did not look quite as beautiful as I remembered. St. Joseph and the Virgin were no longer life-size on their own altars; but when I knelt and said my thanks for kindness shown, the peace and quiet were still there.

I asked the sister who had admitted me whether she could tell me anything about Claire, who had left her classmates to become a nun. "Oh, of course," she replied, "that would be Sister Mary de Lourdes, and certainly she would be so glad to see you." I waited for perhaps ten minutes; maybe someone had to relieve her in the classroom, or wherever her duty was. But suddenly there she was, followed by a silver miniature poodle looking just like my Beau Silver Boy, except that this one was a lady. I would have known Claire anywhere, so little had she changed. The habit was different—it was now a modest street length—and the veil was simplified a bit. We visited for about twenty minutes. There were very few "Do you remembers?" What did we think of the Women's Movement, how did we feel about the changes in her church and my own (the Episcopal church), what about the young people and their different moral and social codes? Then she told me about some of the changes in convent life, how it had become more secular, how some of the young nuns did not even wear veils. "They tell me that the veil is irrelevant," she said, "but my veil is relevant to me." It was relevant to me, too; it, and the women who wore it, held some of my most cherished memories.

NO CHOICE

Shortly before I was to graduate from St. Joseph's Academy I came home from school one day and to my great surprise found a seamstress busily working away in my bedroom. Mother explained to me that I had been accepted by Riverside Hospital to enter their student nurses' probationary class, and that the seamstress was at our house to make my uniforms.

My classmates and I had certainly been thinking and talking about what we would do when we graduated, and I had secretly hoped my stepfather might be willing to pay my tuition at the local business college so that I could prepare myself to become a secretary. Much as I would have loved it, I had pretty well accepted the fact that college was out of the question.

But, a hospital! At that time, I had been, so far as I could recall, in a hospital three times: once to pay my respects to Aunt Ruby in her final illness, again to take some flowers to one of the nuns who had undergone an operation, and the third time to see my friend who had quit school in her junior year to marry and had just had a baby. I had hated the hospital odors and aura of sickness and had made my visits as short as was politely possible. Now it was to become my life. I was appalled.

I suppose Mother felt that anything was better for me than staying in the house of my stepfather, who was so completely restrictive. Maybe she was right. My friends were not welcome, and boys were strictly forbidden. Art lessons had been promised if I would not have a date until I finished high school. Keeping my part of the promise was no problem for me, since my stepfather made it all but impossible for boys to come around. Once one of my classmates who lived not too far from my neighborhood, and who happened to be a boy, showed up with the assigned homework for the next day. I had been absent for a couple of days because of illness. Unfortunately my stepfather had come home from work early and was in the yard. He met the unsuspecting boy at the fence with our large, ferocious-looking Airedale in tow. How was my poor fellow student to know that Dale was the soul of gentleness and would probably welcome a burglar with a warm lick? News of the episode certainly discouraged attention from the opposite sex. My stepfather never kept his part of the promise. I waited until I was forty years old for those lessons, and then my husband paid for them. Certainly no great talent was lost, but the fun of painting has enriched my life and crowded the walls of our home.

Mother tried hard to give Mat and me not only the necessities but also some of the niceties of life. I recall one Saturday matinee when I was taken to see the celebrated actor David Warfield. I can't recall the name of the play, but I still feel the magical excitement of the moment when the house lights went down and the curtains parted to reveal the stage setting. That must be the day I caught stage fever; I have never recovered. Another time we went to see Anna Pavlova dance. She was then in the twilight of her career, but she danced the dying swan, and I cried. Then there were the private schools we attended, some excellent, a couple not too good, but the best the times and the area had to offer, and they were thorough. There were always books given as presents. Mother must have been bone-tired some nights when she read poems to us at bedtime. True, she could not sing, but she had a beautiful speaking voice, low-pitched and rich in timbre.

The years with my stepfather were hard for Mother. Her reasons for the marriage were right, and meant to help her children whom she loved. She just picked the wrong man. Mr. Thomas in his later years, when he and Mother were not divorced but no longer tried to live together, wished to be friends with me. He approved when I married Red, who was a student still in college, and wrote me a letter to that effect. He became proud of his backing when my husband's career began to skyrocket. We took our daughter to see him when she was about a year-and-a-half old, and Mr. Thomas was enchanted with her.

He was a strange man, by turns hard and cold, then charming, and a great raconteur. Often he would entertain us at the dinner table with stories of his experiences as a young man. When I was a boarder at St. Joseph's Academy in St. Augustine and wrote those obligatory weekly letters home, my stepfather would correct the errors and send them back to me. His action infuriated me, but I must admit I never made the same mistake twice. He was, in many ways, the most intellectually stimulating man I ever knew. Certainly he was the most paradoxical.

It was while I was a student nurse at Riverside Hospital that I found out I had become sexually attractive to him. Shortly after I went into training he sold the advertising agency which he had created and owned, and he and Mother moved out to Lynn Haven, a resort community near Panama City in West Florida. He went to be publisher and editor of a weekly newspaper, located I think in Panama City. They kept the house near the hospital in which I had spent my adolescent years, and when Mr. Thomas came back to Jacksonville on business he would stay there. He had on several occasions called the hospital and invited me to meet him at restaurants in town for dinner. It was a treat to have something other than hospital meals, although the food at Riverside was far above average. The break in routine was pleasant, and my stepfather could be interesting company when he chose to be. I was completely unsuspicious when he called one afternoon, saying he was ill at the house and would I come and see him. When I arrived he was in bed, true, but I soon found out he was anything but ill. I was frightened; I was young, barely nineteen; and my rather sheltered upbringing, first in my matriarchal childhood and then with the nuns, had not prepared me for such a situation. But I did have sense enough to leave. I saw to it that I was never again alone in his company. I never told my mother, but I did tell Aunt Ouida. She agreed I must not tell Mother, it would hurt too much.

In his later years, after having owned his own advertising agency and had a fling at being editor and publisher of a newspaper in West Florida, he held a rather minor position with the Florida Agriculture Extension Service. He did some publicity for the Service on WRUF, the university radio station in Gainesville. Last year when my husband and I attended the fiftieth anniversary celebration of the radio station on which Red had, as a student announcer, begun his career, I was surprised to hear the affection with which many of the people present spoke of my stepfather. They called him Uncle Jeff. Obviously he had charmed them! Well, there is a difference between being stepchild and casual friend. It must have been a surprise to my dinner partner who was so warmly remembering "Uncle Jeff" when I suddenly said, "To me he was an S.O.B."

Certainly the years under my stepfather's roof left their mark. I dread the annual start of daylight-saving time. I refuse to serve dinner, no matter how late the hour, until darkness comes; I remember too well those hot six o'clock summertime suppers, served in the bright sunshine, that he demanded. When the meal was finished, my brother and I were sent to our rooms for the night. I read for as long as light remained, then fell asleep. He didn't permit me to turn on the electricity. I suppose Mat did the same.

My stepfather died alone in his sleep in the residential hotel where he had lived his last years. The maid found him when she went to clean his room. I would not have wished that for him.

NURSING—AND A PATIENT

Even though a nursing career had not been my choice, the hospital days proved interesting. The experiences were different and exciting. I like people and was born with an innate desire to please, so I got along well with most patients. I also responded to the drama and demands of the emergency and operating rooms. The delivery room certainly stirred all the woman in me. When I went into training I had never seen, and certainly not touched, a newborn baby, and that first cry still remains the most thrilling single sound I have ever heard. The routine care of bed patients, however, interested me little unless there was a crisis.

During my first experience on night duty as a student at Riverside Hospital a young Episcopal minister was admitted with typhoid. His fever was very high, and I was sent to give him a cold sponge bath. I was very young, barely eighteen, and had never seen a nude man. I managed, under the cover of a sheet, to help him remove his pajamas, but as I turned him over to sponge his back, we both, in our mutual shyness and embarrassment, grabbed for the covering sheet and it wound up tangled in his feet at the foot of the bed. Somehow I got him dry and clothed in clean pajamas, and he went to sleep. That was the last time his temperature went high enough to require a cold sponge bath—heroic measures perhaps?

In a small hospital, as Riverside was at the time I was a student there, the staff becomes almost a family. The hours were long and the work was hard. Private duty shifts were twelve hours and for the duration of the patient's needs, with no time off for Sundays or holidays. I did a little private duty in Jacksonville, after my graduation and while waiting to go to Cook County Hospital in Chicago for postgraduate experience. The set fee was $7 for day duty or $8 for night duty. The nature of the profession left little time or energy for outside contacts, but among my companions I made several rich and lasting friendships.

There are three I recall with real devotion. There was Dr. Jelks, a talented surgeon. His concentration when operating was complete, and he demanded the same from his assistants. We students were in awe of him. In fact, when I had my surgical training and would assist him I was just plain scared, but I admired his sure and rapid skill very much. Later, when I had come back to the hospital as Instructress of Nurses we became good friends. When I announced, at one of the Friday afternoon weekly staff meetings that I was planning to be married, consternation broke loose, with cries to the effect, "There has never been a married staff nurse," and "How will the student nurses react?" Finally Dr. Jelks said in his quick way, "Look, we [meaning the male doctors] are all married, so why can't she be married if she wants to?" Another precedent broken, and no walls came tumbling down. But remember that was 1931.

Another friend I made was Sarah Spears, supervisor of the outpatient department. She visited us several times when we lived in New York, and I am so glad my daughter Sarah was able to know the wonderful woman for whom she was named. When I first met Sarah Spears I was a student nurse and she was *staff*; there was no fraternizing between the two groups. When I had my training in her department, I was near graduation and she was friendly but formal. However, when I returned from Chicago and Cook County Hospital and was staff myself, we soon became friends and she was most helpful. Despite my shiny new Bachelor of Science in nursing, I was unsure of my ability to handle the new job and frightened by the responsibility. Sarah was the person who advised and supported me.

The third person was Dr. T. Z. Cason, who by his friendship and faith in me turned my life around. He was an outstanding internist and at that time one of the three owners of the hospital, along with Dr. Jelks and Dr. Peyton. He taught us students Medical Diseases. He had known my mother when they both were young and was friendly to me from the beginning of my training. Dr. Cason was on the attending staff at the Duval County Hospital, and now and then if I happened to be free he would take me to help him with patients when he had the duty. He was also interested in improving the

Lylah as student nurse, Riverside Hospital, Jacksonville.

quality of nursing education. The Bachelor of Science degree in nursing was his dream and he wanted his hospital, Riverside, to participate in the new project.

Three of the students at Riverside were invited to enter Florida State College for Women at Tallahassee and become part of the five-year course leading to a bachelor's degree in nursing. Dr. Cason chose me as one of the three.

We were really guinea pigs. Neither the hospital nor the college had any guidelines to follow. For some strange reason we were placed in the School of Home Economics. I think that decision must have been crammed down the throat of Dr. Sandals, who was the dean. She was not particularly interested in us, and had no real knowledge of what would be helpful to broaden the medical background that I had begun to get in the period of almost a year that I had already served at Riverside Hospital. I was not asked for my opinion.

I had, of course, the science courses—chemistry, physics, biology—and one year each of history, English, literature, psychology (both normal and abnormal), and a foreign language. For the last I elected French and made the only academic C of my career. C's were routine for my physical education courses, but fortunately there were not enough of them to deprive me of election to Phi Kappa Phi. I resented the home economics courses I was required to take, "Feeding the Family" and such. My roommate was a music major, and I envied her the courses she took in art and philosophy.

There were two highlights in my senior year. The first was Dr. Roger's popular course on Robert Browning's poetry. The other was just the pure satisfaction of getting even. Every home economics major was required to take a seminar course her senior year. Each student presented an hour-long paper on a chosen topic. Can you imagine listening to a solid hour on "Lace Making," or "Saving Steps in the Kitchen," when your degree was to be a B.S. in nursing? My hour finally came, and I presented a paper on "Diagnostic Tests to Determine the Presence of Gonorrhea and Syphilis." This was 1929, and even the words were seldom spoken in polite society. I got my audience's attention.

One happy experience grew out of my constant need to earn spending money. The local newspaper had warm ties with the college and its all-girl student body, and at the suggestion of the feature editor had offered a $5 award and publication for the best sonnet written by a student. I had long been in love with Millay's sonnets, and knew many of them by heart. I entered the contest and won.

Through that contact I met Charles Sloan, the city editor, an attractive man some fifteen years my senior. We were immediately drawn to one another. Here was a "gentleman caller" that my stepfather could not scare away with a large, ferocious-looking dog. Within the confines of the strict college rules covering contact with men we spent much of our free time together. Soon after I graduated he went to the Midwest for a better newspaper job, and I went to Gainesville to join the nursing staff at the university infirmary. It was a happy interlude in my last year at college.

Summer heat and graduation finally came to Tallahassee, and we three guinea pigs, Annie Houstoun, Verna Mae Bouleware, and I, in our caps and gowns, walked proudly onto the stage to receive our Bachelor of Science degrees in nursing, the first three ever given there. I understand that there were two at Yale that year. I do not know of any others. The thing I remember the most about that day was the heat inside those academic gowns. Everyone was stripped to the barest of undergarments beneath. The arrival of a high wind would have been interesting.

I was very happy at college. Finances were difficult but that could not diminish my joy. During my first two years Mother, with some help from my stepfather, paid my room and board, which was $100 a semester. Tuition was equally modest. My beloved aunt Ouida came through with clothes. By my senior year in college I had graduated from training at the hospital and passed the state boards for nurses. I was then a legally registered nurse, and with that credential I was able to get a full scholarship working at the college infirmary. I assisted the physician at his morning office hours and did the simple laboratory tests required in the late afternoon.

For cash in hand I scrounged. Once a student had an emergency appendectomy, and I "specialed" her the first night. For that I got $8. I was so rich that I even went to the tearoom across from the campus and had a decent meal. Another time Dr. Jennie Tilt, the organic chemistry professor (another good friend), was doing an experiment to determine the food value, if any, of the native Florida wild persimmon. For feeding her guinea pigs their varying quotas of

1928 graduating class, Riverside Hospital, including the first three Bachelors of Science in nursing in the state of Florida: Verna Mae Bouleware and Lylah Scarborough (*seated, second and third from left*) and Annie Houstoun (*standing, third from left*).

persimmon, I received thirty-five cents an hour. The International News Service paid me half-a-cent a word for occasional feature stories. It never crossed my mind that I was having a struggle. I was too busy and too happy.

Upon graduation, I was offered the position of Instructress of Nurses at Riverside Hospital, with the proviso that I take a post-graduate course at a large charity hospital to broaden my actual nursing experience. I certainly needed this, since my training had included only paying patients at a small, highly specialized hospital. I had been well trained in the skills that meant comfort and sometimes life itself to the individual patient, but I had almost no administrative experience or knowledge of how to organize the nursing care on large wards of patients.

After some research I chose Cook County Hospital in Chicago. At that time it was the largest charity hospital in the United States, and it certainly offered *experience*. I was accepted for their spring class six months later and was fortunate to get an interim job at the infirmary at the University of Florida in Gainesville. I badly needed the money for train fare to Chicago, and the room-and-board that went with the job was a godsend. The Depression was in full swing by then, and private duty nursing was almost nonexistent.

I had a fine time at the University of Florida. The campus was filled with young men. There was no coeducation then and, except for the head dietitian's daughter, we three nurses were the only young women around. As far as Miss Grimes, the head nurse, would permit, we made the most of the opportunity presented to us.

Saturday nights at the university infirmary during football season were always busy. The stadium was only a block away from the infirmary, and when there was a game there would be injured players, as well as some spectator casualties. The standard nursing schedule then was twelve-hour duty—seven to seven. I was the nurse on duty at night.

One particular Saturday was especially trying. There had been a freshman game that afternoon; the varsity Gators were playing out of town, at Harvard, if I remember correctly. One player had broken an arm, and of course I assisted the doctor in setting it. Another boy had sprained both his wrists and required help for everything and anything. Then, too, four students came in who were very sick. They were from Brooklyn, I think, and to haze them some Florida students who knew better had told them chewing tung nuts was a good laxative. (The University of Florida then was experimenting with tung trees for oil.) It was a laxative all right—a violent laxative. One of the boys had to remain in the infirmary overnight.

All this was added to the duties of an already crowded infirmary filled with some twenty run-of-the-mill patients. It was a horrendous night. Finally I got everybody settled. All medications were administered. The lights were turned low. It was almost midnight. Peace, it was wonderful. I was dead tired. Now I could sit, get off my feet and catch my breath. It had been almost too much.

The doorbell rang. Reluctantly, most reluctantly I answered and opened the door. There stood several students, supporting another, who was a vari-colored mess. He was coated with cake icings—green, pink, yellow—mixed with sand and blood. There had been an accident. A bakery truck had turned over, and this student who was hurt couldn't talk. It was the final straw. All I could do was say, "Take him back . . . and lay him down." That was Red Barber, and he still remembers those first words he heard me say.

The sequence of events that led to his arrival at the infirmary door was as follows. That fall many of the students on football Saturdays would gang up at the downtown motion picture theater for the main showing of the evening, "rush" the theater, and by sheer weight of numbers crash in without paying. The townspeople stopped attending on football Saturday nights. Claude Lee, who ran the theater, offered the students a deal: Don't "rush" my paying shows, and at eleven o'clock every football Saturday night I'll give you a full show, plus extra short subjects. You can bring your dates, and own the theater.

Red and Jerry Carter shared a small apartment. The Depression was on, and both of them were working their way through school. Red waited tables. Jerry had a job selling bakery goods; he went to Jacksonville, filled a truck with cakes and other items, and peddled them to the Gainesville stores. He had gotten a fresh load that afternoon. Several friends dropped by the apartment, and to help during the long wait for the free show somebody suggested going down the road and getting some shine whiskey. (These were Prohibition days.) They all piled into the truck, which somehow turned over. Red got coated with various icings, and part of the truck hit his back.

It wasn't until the next day that he got completely cleaned up. He wasn't badly hurt. He spent the weekend at the infirmary, and went to his Monday classes. He returned late that afternoon with a box of long-stemmed roses. I was hooked.

Thereafter, when I was fortunate enough to have an evening off-duty, we walked to the duck pond between the infirmary building and the stadium. It was an attractive wooded area and fairly secluded. After that long twelve-hour on-duty shift, I was tired and my feet hurt. I would often take off my shoes, and Red would rub my feet and sing to me in his pleasing tenor voice. I still remember the words of one song:

> They still believe in old Japan
> Should lovers live their earthly span
> Without fulfillment of desire
> Or leave unquenched love's sacred fire,
> They'll live again to love at last
> When ten thousand years have passed.
>
> Ten thousand years is a long, long time
> To wait for a dream to come true.
> It would seem just a day
> Dreaming centuries away
> To wake at the end with you.

Among our friends were Judy and Hampton Jarrell. Hampton was a young English instructor, and Red was one of his pupils. Because Red had worked a couple of years after high school before going to college, teacher and pupil were not far apart in age. Judy would invite us to come for coffee and dessert in the evening. She was learning to cook and would practice one dish until she was satisfied with it. We had quite a run on lemon meringue pie, but her finished product still remains the best one I've ever tasted. After dessert and a short visit Hampton would announce that he had papers to grade, and he and Judy would say good-night and retreat to their bedroom, leaving us the living room. How blessed with friends we have been through the years.

I spent that Christmas academic break in Tampa with Aunt Ouida. Red's parents were also living there, and he took me to meet them. Mrs. Barber, who was by then an invalid, so small and frail, sat by the fire in the living room. She made me most welcome and told me that her son was like his father, who had been helpful with the three children in the years when she was first teaching and then was principal of the new elementary school in Sanford. She made me feel that she liked me. Red's father, who was a locomotive engineer, did the same. In fact, in his warm, well-modulated Southern voice, he told me, "If Walter ever gives you any trouble, just let me know and I'll come straighten him out." He meant it. He was always on my side—and he called me Murray. I liked that.

I left the visit with the feeling that Red had told them we were serious and that they welcomed the news.

My mother, by contrast, took a dim view of my romance with a student who was working his way through college. That he certainly was doing. He was a janitor at a bachelor professors' club, where he was given a room. For meals, he waited tables at Ma Troumper's off-campus restaurant. Our few treats, largely cups of coffee after our private walks, came from the money he sometimes won when he played bridge with the professors. For me to have offered to share the cost would have offended his pride, and not seemed quite proper to me. In 1929 girls did not share expenses on dates.

A few weeks before I was to leave for Cook County Hospital in Chicago, Red was given the opportunity to work part-time at WRUF, the university radio station on campus. The young boy whose ambition had been to be an end-man in a minstrel show and had traveled in his freshman year with the glee club was now a special performer, doing a one-man minstrel act. He had his foot in the door! His lifelong love affair with show business had begun.

Mother could not know or understand. Her father and husband had both been lawyers, and to her that was a proper profession for a young man. She probably would have been pleased had I told her that he had entered law school. When I did inform her that I was planning to marry Red after I returned from Chicago, she was not only surprised, she was distressed. She said, "Well, at least stop calling him by that silly nickname—call him by his proper name." I had to stop and think before I could tell Mother that his name was Walter. I still call him Red, as do millions of people. Aside from his

parents, I've rarely heard him called Walter. Two men always did—
Red Smith, the famed sports columnist, and Branch Rickey, whom
my husband loved as though he were a second father.

All too soon the time came for me to board the train for Chicago
and the Great Adventure. By then Red and I knew we wanted to
spend our lives together. It was a wrench to leave him. It was also
hard to go alone to a strange city and to a charity hospital.

STRANGE NEW WORLD

When I got on the train in Jacksonville to go to Chicago, I had never been further north than Atlanta, Georgia, where I had visited once with Dannie in my early childhood, nor further south of Jacksonville than Fort Pierce, where as a little girl I had spent a summer vacation with Aunt Fanny.

Even though the economic situation, except for the few years with my stepfather, had been difficult, there had been family, then the gentle nuns, and always friends to ease the going and to reassure me. Now I was completely on my own, and more than a little frightened. But I was excited, too, and ready for the challenge.

The Chicago where I stepped off the platform of the train and into was lawless and gangster-ridden. Al Capone was at the height of his reign. The city was close to bankruptcy and was meeting its payrolls only intermittently; during the six months I was there it seldom did. The Nurses' Home was housed in rooms of old brownstone houses, and the hospital was, to me, enormous. I was suddenly in another world. When I went to bed my first night in the room that had been assigned to me, I put my clothes on a chair under the window and opened it wide. I awakened the next morning to a white world, and my clothes were sprinkled with snow, the first snow I had ever seen. Once in my childhood in Jacksonville a few flakes fell, but they melted before they hit the ground. For the next five months in Chicago almost everything I saw or did was a "first."

My initial assignment was to Children's Hospital. It was the newest building in the complex, and it sort of eased me into what the old wards in the adult hospital would be like. Even so, I was not prepared for the children's venereal disease ward, or for a ward filled with mongoloids and other birth-marred babies. My first patient was a fourteen-year-old black boy. He was also my first black patient. He had typhoid fever and we were in isolation together for almost two weeks. He was hostile and I was frightened; but somehow I managed to cope, and finally he recovered and went home.

Most of the doctors and nurses had never seen a case of typhoid before. I was in my element here. At least this was not a first; every summer in Jacksonville we expected and were prepared for a few cases. I still remember those icy cold sponges to bring down the frightening high temperatures, but they must have been a shock to the patient.

When I was at Cook County the "unit system," I believe it was called, was in vogue. A nurse was assigned a particular chore, and she repeated that one procedure for eight long hours every day until her assignment was changed. It could be deadly dull—pouring and passing medicines all day, for example. I spent one week on the obstetrical ward doing nothing but pumping breasts to get milk for premature or sick babies. I almost lost my mind, but I did learn much about the lives of poor women in Chicago. Visitors were not allowed on the obstetrical ward, and the women who could give milk, over what their own babies needed or sometimes because their own babies had not lived, were glad to have someone other than a patient in the next bed to visit with.

The surgical wards were full of drama. There were always "gunshot wounds" being admitted. The gang wars were in their heyday and not only the participants but the innocent bystanders caught in the crossfire were victims. When doing admissions we were coached to examine body and clothing for bullets, and to be sure any found were saved for the police. Occasionally members of the staff or members of their families would be admitted for surgery. Once the young wife of an intern, who had been in an automobile accident, was brought in, and I was assigned to "special" her. There happened to be a small room with only two beds in it, off the big ward, and she was put in one of them. I did enjoy the chance, and the time, to practice the pleasing skills I had been taught at Riverside Hospital.

Not all of my time was taken up by work in the hospital or attendance at lectures given by the outstanding attending staff. There was the city to explore, my first elevated train to ride, and beautiful Lake

Michigan to walk or ride the bus along. There were many young men with whom I had a few dates, but I wasn't really interested. In fact, my conversation had such a single theme that my new women friends teased me and called me "Red says." I loved the Art Museum, on Lake Michigan, and that summer I saw and heard my first opera at Ravinia Park. It was so cold that I wore my Florida winter coat. How quickly that Chicago weather changed when the wind blew in off the lake.

When my time was up at Cook County, I was offered two positions. One was to teach on the Nursing School staff. The other was to be an assistant to Miss Harding, who was supervisor of Women's Surgical, where I had nursed the intern's wife. Miss Harding had assigned me because she said I knew how to take care of a private patient. You can bet I did, after my years at Riverside Hospital.

I was tempted. It was flattering to be offered not one but two jobs. To work with Miss Harding would be pleasant; she was by far the most attractive member of the nursing staff that I had met. On the other hand, to be on the staff of the prestigious Nursing School would relieve me of the routine of patient nursing care, which can become monotonous.

I had been gone from Florida for six months, and I found the city of Chicago exciting, offering opportunities that certainly did not exist in Jacksonville, Florida, which was still a small city. Did I really want to marry Red, or for that matter was I ready to marry anyone and give up the independence I had worked hard to achieve? There was only one way to find out. I turned my face South and came back home.

Late that summer, after my post-graduate work at Cook County Hospital was finished, another student and I boarded a Greyhound bus. It was around five in the afternoon that the long ride home began. Her destination was Macon, Georgia, and mine was Jacksonville, Florida. The night seemed endless; there were many stops at small towns with dirty restrooms. Sleep was almost impossible. This was 1930; times were hard, money was scarce, and the bus was the cheapest way to get home. It had seemed a fine idea when we left

Chicago, but by about four o'clock the next afternoon, as we were nearing Chattanooga, Tennessee, we both decided that come hell or high water we must have a night's sleep in a bed that wasn't moving. The Greyhound office was in a hotel lobby. We gathered our luggage, went to the office, and got refunds for the unused part of the trip. With great expectations we prepared to check into the hotel. Well, there was no high water, but the American Legion was holding its convention in Chattanooga and there wasn't an available room in town.

By now the bus had departed and the lobby was fast filling with Legionnaires and noise. There was no choice but to resume our journey by train. I bought a lower berth; my companion elected to continue her shorter journey by coach. I telegraphed home my change in arrival time. Since that night I have stayed in many of the famous hotels of the world, and have sailed the Atlantic and Pacific oceans in the finest first-class staterooms, but nothing has looked as beautiful to me as that lower berth on the Pullman did on that hot evening in Chattanooga.

Next morning, as the train drew nearer and nearer to my destination, I began to have qualms. Was I ready to make a lifetime commitment to someone I had not seen for six months? Was I in love with a man or an idea? Suddenly, with a sense of near panic, I wondered whether he would still love me. Would he even be there when the train stopped? As the engine slowed I looked out the window, and there Red stood, waiting on the platform. The six months vanished.

Mother did not come to meet the train. I still don't know why. Did she give us our private moment of reunion, even though she opposed the courtship, or was it her lifetime distaste for any activity that took place before ten o'clock in the morning?

There were a few days in which to find living quarters near the hospital. My friend Helen de Montmollen and I took a room in the home of George and Lois Treisback, only two blocks from the hospital. Helen and I had gone through college and training together and we enjoyed the arrangement. At the time she was working in the outpatient department at Riverside Hospital.

After five years and six months of preparation I waited with antici-pation and some apprehension for September and the beginning of the academic year. Now I would no longer be student nurse, but staff, with the impressive title of Instructress of Nurses.

The Riverside Hospital to which I returned was quite small. A few rooms had been added on the top floor, which in my student days had housed only the x-ray department. There was a new supervisor of nurses. Otherwise the staff were the people I had known as a student, and that was reassuring. Despite my shiny new Bachelor of Science in nursing, I was not sure of my ability to handle the new job and frightened by the responsibility. It was Sarah Spears, supervisor of the outpatient department, who guided me through the rough spots. Now that we were both staff, she became the close friend of our free hours and she was so much fun. When our weekends off duty coincided we would often get into her car and drive down to Gainesville, where her sister was housemother for one of the frater-nities and my dear Red was working at the university radio station. She approved of my young man and did all she could to further the romance. We stayed in touch through the years, and I made the trip from Miami to be with her when the hospital honored her on the fiftieth anniversary of its founding. She died a few weeks later. I still miss her.

MRS. WALTER LANIER BARBER

Seven months later, in the living room of the Treisback home, Red and I were married. Lois gave us a reception, even though she was at the time recovering from the birth of her third daughter, Paula, who was only four weeks old. The staff doctors and nurses who were not actually on duty came. Cousin Eula brought my grandmother Dannie, dressed in her best, and so delighted to be present. Major and Mrs. Garland Powell (he was Red's boss at the University of Florida radio station and had gotten him the raise that made it possible for us to dare to get married) drove up from Gainesville and brought the groom and his roommate Jimmy Butsch. Later Jimmy would follow us to Cincinnati and become first an announcer and later an executive with the Crosley Corporation. Professor Hauptman, who had a car, rare in those Depression days, brought the best man, Frank DeGaetani, who was also a professor. Dr. Jennie Tilt came from my college in Tallahassee. I had met her when she was a patient at the hospital and I was young in my training. I was assigned to give her the routine daily care. We became friendly over her morning bed-bath. Later, when I went to Tallahassee for the college portion of my training she was encouraging and would arrange little treats. It was she who recommended me to her college sorority, Kappa Alpha Theta, which I enjoyed and which has been such a help to me in my married years when my husband's career has taken him to different parts of the country. There were always Thetas to welcome me and help in adjustment to the new city.

My mother, who was so distressed at my determination to marry the young part-time student/part-time broadcaster, refused to say she would be at the service. Perhaps I can understand now, but I certainly did not then. She had gone shopping with me when I bought my wedding dress, and though she did not enthuse she was not openly hostile. I was surprised when she said she didn't believe that she and my brother would come. My immediate reaction was one of anger. As I write this I'm still angry. Did she really think that at the last moment she could make me change my mind, or did she just resent my happiness?

It was Lois Treisback who phoned her the night before and pleaded with Mother to come, telling her that if she didn't she would always be sorry. Perhaps Mother was waiting to be urged, for she and my brother arrived just minutes before the time for the ceremony. It made me very happy, and I am still grateful to Lois for her intervention. So was Mother, though she could never say so. Later Mother lived with us for much of the time in our New York years, particularly when my brother was in Europe in combat in the World War II days. Red was always good to her. They became real friends. She once said to me, not long before she died, "I love him more than I love either one of my own children."

Red's parents were not able to come. His mother was seriously ill and unable to travel. She died on New Year's Eve that same year.

Dr. Cason had given us the rental of a car for a wedding present, and after the reception we departed in a big shiny Franklin automobile for our three-day honeymoon in Charleston, South Carolina. No two people were ever richer or happier. We drove all the way to Savannah, Georgia, before we discovered the tin cans tied on the back of the car. We stopped to spend the night at Savannah, and when I opened my grip to take out the dress I was wearing to dinner, rice scattered all over the floor. George Treisback had added that touch. Times were hard but our friends were generous in their gifts and thoughtfulness.

Shortly after our marriage Miss Traxler, who was supervisor of nurses, became ill and had to resign. I was asked to take the position until a permanent person could be found. The change meant I had to live in the Nurses' Home, where it was impossible for Red to stay when he would come up from Gainesville for the once-a-week sports program he was doing for a local radio station. My weekends, which had been relatively free when I was teaching, were seriously curtailed. Red was growing tired of being, as my student nurses called him, "Miss Scarborough's husband"—and a part-time husband at

Red Barber, at microphone in Gainesville.

that. I was relieved when the new supervisor arrived and I could go to Gainesville to live and become a full-time wife.

In early December, 1931, I joined Red in the apartment he had rented in the home of Mrs. Lartigue, who was the widow of a physician. It was roomy and private, and we happily settled in and began planning our first married Christmas.

Mrs. Lartigue was a truly elegant lady. She was tall and slender, with a mass of white hair and vivid blue eyes. Her face was beautiful, and her grooming was at all times impeccable. She was politely kind but formal. I was younger than both her daughters, but for the months we lived there I remained "Mrs. Barber." Some of our Saturday night parties must have gotten pretty noisy. White lightning, as Dad Williams' bootleg product was called, flowed freely, but if we kept her awake she never made a complaint. Every afternoon in the hot summer months, Mrs. Lartigue would appear about five o'clock, formally dressed including white cotton gloves, unwind the garden hose, and water the hanging baskets of blooming petunias on the porch and in the flower beds in the front yard. It was done with all the grace and formality of a lady pouring tea at the governor's mansion.

We grieved when her daughter Marie's husband was transferred back to Gainesville and we had to move out and give possession to the rightful owners. From Mrs. Lartigue's we moved to a one-bedroom apartment on the second floor of the McKinstry home, a beautiful antebellum house. It sat in the middle of a large garden, only a block off the main street along which the trains ran through town. A garden path led through the front yard to a verandah opening into a wide center hall with a beautiful stairway at the far end. Halfway up was a landing with a window looking on the garden. It was like my grandmother Scarborough's house, only much larger and more elegant. Miss Belle lived there with her younger sister Miss Janey and their mother, who was well into her nineties. Miss Belle was our landlady, and at the time taught in the public school.

Our apartment consisted of a living room, a tiny kitchen, a bathroom even smaller, and our very spacious bedroom which opened onto the upstairs verandah. Both living room and bedroom had fireplaces, which were our only means of heating the apartment in the winter, except for a small oil burner in the bathroom. Miss Belle's niece Miriam and her husband, who was a professor at the university, had a room and bath across the hall. Sometimes our friend Jimmy lived there also. As I think back, the material was certainly there for another novel by William Faulkner. There were the maiden ladies, Miss Belle and Miss Janey, well past middle age, the ancient mother, and the beautiful old house grown shabby from lack of money to keep it up. Miss Belle, as far as I could observe, was the only source of income. Miss Janey kept house in a very vague sort of way, and was eccentric to the point of being queer. The old lady, Mrs. McKinstry, spent most of her time in a rocking chair on the front porch. Now and then, on my way inside I would stop and visit with her. Her abiding passion was not to live to be one hundred years old. She once said to me, with feeling, "I will not live to be one hundred!" She didn't.

I felt sad for the two sisters. They were typical of the large number of maiden ladies prevalent at that time in the Deep South. They lived out their lives in the homes of their married brothers and sisters, little more than housekeepers and nurses for the children of their more fortunate relatives. The third sister, mother of Miriam, had escaped into marriage, but she died early, leaving Miss Belle and Miss Janey to raise her daughter. Such women were the inheritors of the terrible decimation of the young men of the South by the Civil War and the impoverishment of the Reconstruction years that followed. Not always were they by choice maiden ladies.

The two-and-a-half years we lived in Gainesville were busy ones and on the whole happy. Two strong-minded, ambitious young people were learning how to live, peaceably most of the time, with their differences. The young boy who had wanted to be an end-man in a minstrel show had found his profession in the newest facet of show business: radio. He was busy learning, working hard to improve his skills, broadcasting the games of the university football and town baseball teams. These were seasonal—just parts of a full schedule in the studio which ran the gamut from a live country music band to the "Hour with the Masters," a recorded program of symphony concerts and grand opera. The demanding routine was a fine opportunity for a young person to find out what he could do. His vacations, and what little extra money we could spare, Red spent looking for a better job. He rode buses at night (no hotel bills) and took auditions in the day. His itinerary included WSB in Atlanta, WHAS in Louisville, and WLW in Cincinnati, at that time the most powerful radio station in the world, 500,000 watts.

I was learning how to cook and keep house and, when it was available, doing a little private duty and filling in for Dr. Thomas' office nurse when she had a vacation. The work was a godsend, bringing in a little of the extra money we badly needed.

Our entertainment was our friends, young professors and their wives, college mates of mine who were married and living in Gainesville, and bachelor companions of Red's college days. We played bridge and on Saturday nights gathered at someone's apartment for a party featuring communal food and Dad Williams' shine.

The last home Red and I had in Gainesville was a little two-bedroom cottage we rented for $35 a month one block off the university campus. The Joe Wilsons, who were friends of ours (I had nursed her in the hospital when their son was born), were moving from their rather spacious house into a small apartment and they needed a place to store part of their furniture. They offered us the loan of some of their living-room chairs and a table. On the strength of that promise we went down to the local furniture store, bought a double bed and a bureau, as well as a dinette table and four chairs, all on monthly installment payments, and rented the house. We felt quite elegant, even though our kitchen stove was a two-burner gas plate. A small hood could be placed over one burner to make an oven of sorts. It did very well, as far as my newly learned cooking skills went anyway. Jimmy Butsch wanted to move in with us, so we furnished the other bedroom for him.

Alas, our new affluence lasted only a short time. After a few months the Wilsons found that with a fast-growing little boy the apartment was crowded, or perhaps the people who rented their house left town or couldn't pay the rent; I don't really remember. But I do remember they took back their furniture, and we were left with an empty living room. We bought several unpainted outdoor chairs with striped canvas covers and lots of cans of dark green enamel paint. After our labors we thought them quite handsome. Two citrus packing-crates, with some more of that green paint, became coffee table and bookcase. Fortunately the room was small and we felt we had handled the challenge quite well. It didn't look too different from the apartments our friends had rented. We thought it had more style and we had our privacy. There was no one to complain about late hours or noise. We were the only ones of our group who were not living either with in-laws or in an apartment. It was not surprising that our house soon became the accepted gathering place for our Saturday nights. It was agreed that the other wives

would bring the food. We provided ice and coffee and cleaned up on
Sunday morning. The cost of Dad Williams' liquid refreshment was
prorated. The arrangements suited us just fine. We had more energy
than money, even though those Sunday mornings brought reality
back with a bang.

Shortly after our move to the little house I fell heir to a regular
job—manna from heaven in those Depression days. Franklin D.
Roosevelt had been elected president in November of 1932 and took
office in March of 1933. Almost immediately he established the
Works Progress Administration, quickly shortened to the W.P.A. Its
purpose was to create jobs among all levels of the population. As a
university town, Gainesville had a large number of professional
people out of work because of the Depression. The project was
aimed at them, as well as at giving some nutritional help to the primary school-aged children of the poverty-stricken tenant farmer
families in the surrounding county. They came to school on the bus.
Many had gone without any breakfast. The project was to supply
them with a hot breakfast and have their physical condition checked
by the school nurse, and, when needed, by the public health doctor.
The doctor routinely had the children examined for hookworm and
malaria parasites, common among them.

This was where I came into the picture. Because of my professional training I became laboratory technician for the project. The
work took my morning hours, but most of the time I was free from
noon on. Louise Kincaid, who was school nurse, and I became
friends, and I enjoyed the work. Occasionally when some of the children involved in the program were ill and unable to come to school,
or were badly undernourished, Louise and I would get in her car and
take milk out to their homes. I remember my shock when I would
see, sitting on the kitchen table, the container of milk left the day
before still unopened. Once I saw a mother chewing crackers from a
box of ginger snaps, reducing them to a gruel consistency in her
mouth and feeding it with her fingers to her nursing baby. Where

could one begin to try to lift them from the inertia brought on by their poverty, ignorance, and poor health?

Louise tried hard for them. She was concerned and kind, but it was all uphill. I remember once when she had gotten a dental appointment for a child whose teeth were badly in need of attention. She went where the father worked part-time as a handyman to arrange for him to take his daughter for her appointment. It was not Louise's first contact with him; the school was well supplied with Mr. Peacock's children. His reply was short and to the point: "Miss Kincaid, that's your problem." The doctor would tease her and say, "Miss Kincaid, you can beg the blankets and give them to them, but you can't go around every night and cover them up." I wonder whether she finally gave up trying.

PART TWO

NORTH

QUICK AS LIGHTNING

There came a day—March 4, 1934—when I walked home from work, opened the front door, and saw, standing in the middle of the living room, an open trunk filled with my husband's clothes. I was stunned. I ran into the bedroom, and opened the closet and his dresser drawers. Not even a handkerchief remained. I was alternately tearful and furious with anger. I couldn't understand. When Red arrived a little later he was greeted with cold silence. I remember thinking once while I waited, "At least he didn't take 'my' wardrobe trunk," a relic of college days. His explanation was immediate and, when I cooled down enough to take it in, great news. Those rough night rides on buses, the auditions taken, and the hard-to-spare money spent on his job-hunting trips had paid off. Shortly after I had left for work a telegram had arrived from Chet Thomas, supervisor of announcers at WLW, Cincinnati. (Red had taken an audition there the previous summer and had been promised a job only to have it cancelled because of the worsening economic depression.) The telegram read: "Will you do Cincinnati Reds games twenty-five dollars a week?" Red wired back, "Yes." An hour or so later the next telegram came: "Report tomorrow Scotty Reston, Tampa Florida." Scotty was then road secretary for the ball club. Today readers of the *New York Times* know him as James Reston, the distinguished political columnist.

Powell Crosley, who owned the Crosley Radio Corporation, had bought the Cincinnati club and was of course going to broadcast his club's games on WSAI, companion station to his powerful WLW. Later, when Red asked how he happened to be chosen, Chet Thomas told him the story. When the decision to broadcast the games was made, he and John Clarke, then general manager, discussed who should be the announcer. Chet put Red's name in the pot. Clarke said, "Oh, that's the young man from Florida, the one in the white linen suit, who came up for an audition. I remember he said he did sports. Send for him." That blessed white linen suit! Opportunity had knocked, and Red answered.

He left on the bus the next morning for Tampa. He had a week there to become acquainted with the club, and then went to Cincinnati to work as a studio announcer until the season began. As soon as he had an address I sent him that trunk. When I first saw it I had asked where he got it, and he said he had made a deal with Cox Furniture Company. At the end of the month they got the furniture we were buying on installment, and, for our equity in it, Red got the trunk. How kind they were. They were just glad Red had gotten his chance.

My godmother Mrs. Jordan offered me the use of a spare bedroom in her home. It was the same house I had played in as a child when she would take me home after Sunday church during the time I was in Miss Maggie's school. I had spent happy hours there with her two children, Esther and Birkett. I felt secure there. I was busy between my job and closing the little cottage. I had my safe room to go to at night and Mrs. Jordan to make me feel welcome.

It was not too lonely while I waited for Red to feel financially secure enough for me to join him. I sold or gave away the few pieces of furniture that did not belong to the furniture store. The wardrobe trunk from my college and training school days had gone to Mrs. Jordan's. It held my clothes, our sterling silver, the three lovely pewter pieces from Red's father and mother, the four pewter goblets from Aunt Ouida, and the electric clock from Red's best man, all of them wedding presents. The electric clock has been faithful. It sits on my work table now as I write these memoirs over fifty years later.

When the truck was loaded with the furniture to go back to the store there remained only one thing in the empty house, a cardboard box of Christmas tree ornaments. I gave them to the driver.

The wait was not too long. Red got a raise and sent the money for my train fare. I bought a new dress to travel in, and I was on my way. I could not know then, as I settled in my seat on the train, how different my life would now become. Except for the time in Chicago I had lived in the Deep South with family and friends close by. The rituals of life would be shaken and changed—no more meetings with friends for a mid-morning Coke at the drugstore, no afternoon bridge games with the other young wives. The people I would meet would be mostly midwesterners, some of whom would mock my accent. My leisure time and companions would be determined by the demands of my husband's profession. I was moving into the world of show business. But all of that was in the future. I was filled with happiness. I only cared that we would soon be together again.

I have never been, in the generally accepted sense of the word, a "sports fan." The world of my early childhood was entirely ma-triarchal. My mother and my two grandmothers were all widows. The summer I spent with Aunt Mollie and Cousin Eula in the village of Boston, Georgia, Aunt Mollie's husband owned a store in a nearby town and was only home on Sundays. The modest tennis games at the Diocesan School and St. Joseph's Academy were just required exercise. I had long since discovered the joy of reading. How could a game compete with Poe's "The Fall of the House of Usher"?

I had graduated from Florida State College for Women with my B.S. in nursing and was working at the University of Florida Infirm-ary before I became introduced to the manly sports of football and baseball. Rosa Grimes, who was head nurse at the infirmary, was a football fan, and the players soon learned that she was a soft spot for a meal of goodies not found on the training table. For the three young women who did the actual nursing, football season meant an increase in broken bones and sprains. I enjoyed the young players and began to learn the rules of the game. I even saw a couple of the freshmen games, my first exposure to football. Rosa Grimes went to the varsity games.

That same fall I met the person I was to marry a year and a half later. He wasn't a football player or a sports announcer. He was a full-time student majoring in English literature and planning to be a college professor.

When I returned from Chicago to begin my position as In-structress of Nurses in the late summer of 1930 at Riverside Hospital in Jacksonville, Red was no longer a student. Times were hard. Florida had been hit by the national depression early and severely. The $100 that Red had saved from the odd jobs, mostly day labor, at which he had worked the two years following graduation from high school, was exhausted. He was hanging on by the sort of thing available to students—waiting tables for meals, being the janitor in a bachelor professors' club for a room, and working in the university library for money. The going wage at that time was thirty-five cents an hour. He had also done some part-time work at the university radio station.

When Major Powell, who was station manager, offered him a position on the staff provided he would quit college and work full-time, he grabbed at the opportunity. The backing of our combined salaries made it possible for us to get married, even though we knew that until my obligation to the hospital was satisfied, I would be living in Jacksonville and he in Gainesville.

By the time I came to Gainesville, Ralph Nimmons, who had been chief announcer when Red was hired, had quit to go to a larger radio station up north. My husband inherited the job. This meant he did everything—an afternoon hour of classical music (records, of course), the news, emcee for the Orange Grove String Band, hillbilly (including him singing the lyrics), and interviews with university professors on various academic subjects.

All of this I had expected, but the big surprise was soon to come. I had, indeed, married a sports broadcaster after all. WRUF was a state-owned radio station and the University of Florida was a state institution and, to a large extent, legislatively controlled. All of the university's athletic programs were expected to be aired over WRUF. They included football, baseball, swimming meets, amateur boxing, golf, northeast Florida semi-pro baseball, and state high school basketball finals. Those finals were gruelling, beginning in the early morning and continuing until late afternoon without even a lunch break. I think Red's tepid appreciation for basketball began the day he broadcast those games. I, on the other hand, enjoy watching it a bit now and then. The game seems to me to have some of the grace of ballet done in double tempo.

Since it was becoming increasingly evident that the part of the work Red enjoyed most and did best was the various sports events, and because the world of athletics would be a major part of my life, I thought I had best begin learning as much as I could about that alien world. I went, of course, to the athletic events on campus, not only to widen my education but also because they were free. The football seats came to Red courtesy of the athletic department. Our combined incomes certainly contained no amusement fund. I even went to a prize fight called, I think, the Small Town Fight Club. The only thing I remember about it was that the police chief's wife and I were the only women there.

My first year in Cincinnati I saw many of the games. I had a pass next to the row of seats on the mezzanine where Red did his broadcasts. A five-cent ride on the streetcar and my pass got me into the game. The price was right.

After our daughter's birth, I did not go to many games. I was busy learning to be a mother and to care for a growing infant. I always felt welcome at Crosley Field when Larry MacPhail and Warren Giles were general managers. I was pleased when the Reds won. It made a more interesting broadcast for my husband and a happier afternoon for MacPhail and Giles, both of whom were personal friends. I enjoyed watching certain players exercise their polished skills. But a fan, no. There was never a player or his wife who was a guest in our home. Red had made that a rule at the beginning of his career, so that there could never be a claim of favoritism.

A fan—no. I do not own players' pictures, nor do I have a well-worn sweatshirt once worn by Eddie Stanky, as does my friend Ann Honeycutt.

The apartment to which Red took me was small, really only a one-room efficiency, but it was in a brand-new building in Clifton, a well-established, tree-shaded residential section of Cincinnati within walking distance of the radio station. We were the first occupants of our apartment, and I was more intrigued than dismayed by the fact that one set of double doors in the living room opened into a pullman kitchen and the other hid a pull-down double bed, neither of which I had ever seen before. It was attractively furnished, and the bath was spacious, with both tub and shower. There were a few one-bedroom apartments, but most were like ours and, because of size and location, filled with young people, many of them from the radio station. It was rather like a superior college dormitory with no restrictions. We lived there happily until another raise made more spacious quarters possible.

Opening Day, 1934, with its citywide excitement came a few days after my arrival, but I didn't see it. It was and still is a tradition that Cincinnati play the first game of the new season at home, because the first professional major league team had been set up in Cincinnati in 1869. I stayed by the radio in the apartment so that I could tell Red how his broadcast went. Lon Warneke pitched a one-hit shutout for the Chicago Cubs, and that hit came in the ninth inning. Red almost had a no-hit game for his debut.

The first summer in Cincinnati, while we were still living in the small apartment, the city had a record-breaking heat wave. For eight days and nights the temperature did not go below 100°. I can still feel the heat on the day the thermometer hit 108°. In 1934 air conditioning was practically unknown. Only two places in Cincinnati had it, the big theater downtown and Mabley and Carew, a department store.

Our small quarters had no cross-ventilation. We bought an electric fan and a large galvanized washtub which we kept filled with ice at the foot of the bed. The fan we set so it blew over the tub—a crude sort of air conditioning, but something. With the help of repeated cold showers we got a little sleep and made it through the nights.

Clifton, the section of town where we were living, was on a hill. Down in the basin of the Ohio River in the crowded tenements it was another story. People spread newspapers on the ground in the public parks (Cincinnati has many beautiful ones) and slept there. During the course of the ordeal a woman in the basin picked up a beer bottle and hit her husband repeatedly on the head. He died of brain injury. When she was brought before the judge he pointed out to her that she had a good reputation with her neighbors, had never been in trouble with the law, and got along well with her husband. He asked her, "Why did you do it?" Her reply was short and tragic: "Your honor, it was so hot I just had to do something." The whole town understood. People were glad when she was declared "not guilty because of temporary insanity" and sent to a hospital.

One summer a few years later when our daughter was about eight years old she and I were back in Cincinnati for a short visit with her godfather and his family. When we stepped off the train in the late afternoon the temperature was 104°. Sarah said in a panicky voice, "Mother, it's too hot here, let's get back on the train." I have never experienced, even in the Deep South, anything to compare with a heat wave in the Ohio River Valley . . . and without air conditioning.

Other new experiences came crowding in. Cincinnati has always been a city with a strong feeling for good music—perhaps it came with the first settlers, who were largely of Germanic origin. We waited, with pleasant anticipation, our first fall for the opening of the Cincinnati Symphony concert season. My husband, in our courting days, had introduced me to the joy of symphonic music through records at the radio station. Claude Murphree, who was the official organist for the University of Florida and a good friend, had taken us to a performance of the Minneapolis Symphony under the baton of Eugene Ormandy.

With great excitement we boarded the streetcar—it cost five cents each—for our first Sunday afternoon concert in our new hometown. Eugene Goossens was conducting the Cincinnati Symphony. We paid twenty-five cents each for tickets and began our climb to our seats in the "peanut gallery." When we arrived we discovered that we would be sitting next to a black couple. Hastily, but quietly with our carefully taught Southern prejudice intact, we moved to still higher seats in the last row of the gallery, which was unoccupied. I didn't hear much of the music. I was too busy examining myself and my own emotions. I watched the black couple down below, who were unaware of my turmoil, obviously enjoying the music. By the end of the concert I reluctantly accepted the knowledge that my reaction had only hurt me.

I never felt quite the same again. Absurdity had cracked the wall of prejudice. The child of the South had taken a first step toward becoming a citizen of the world. Looking back, I see that it was a preparation for Red. He was the principal announcer for the Brooklyn Dodgers when thirteen years later Branch Rickey broke the color line with Jackie Robinson.

THE WORLD OF BASEBALL

For most people the new year begins on January 1. Not so in the world of baseball, which had now become my world. Everything starts fresh with spring training. There are young rookies to be tried out and tested, fading stars getting in shape for "just one more year," friends to be greeted after the winter separation. For the wives who are not kept home by the needs of children in school it is also a special time to be with their husbands before the long season begins of half of the time at home, half on the road. My first spring training was exciting; it was all so different from the world in which I had grown up. I had never seen a baseball game until after my marriage.

During my thirty-three years in the world of major league baseball, life took on much of its color from the personalities of the general managers of the three clubs with which Red was associated— first with the Cincinnati Reds, then the Brooklyn Dodgers, and finally the New York Yankees. The general manager of a major league ball club is a person of unique power, unless the dominant role is taken by an owner such as the O'Malleys, Walter and Peter, of the Dodgers, or George Steinbrenner of the Yankees. The general manager answers only to the owner. The field manager, coaches, and scouts are of his choosing. It is his responsibility to find the promising young players and judge whether they are ready to come to the majors. He also must make the hard decision as to when a player's useful days are over. He hires and fires. He sets the tone of the whole endeavor. This is particularly true during the period of spring training, when everyone in the organization is together in a fairly isolated environment.

Larry MacPhail was Red's first general manager. When we came to Cincinnati he was forty-four years old, a handsome red-headed Scotsman, loud, explosive, but full of charm, and I was captivated. In those early days of radio, long before television, arrangements for broadcasting the games were simple. The press occupied a box in the upper stands behind home plate. Red and his engineer used the adjoining box, and I sat in the box next to them.

For streetcar fare I could ride from our apartment to the ball park, and with the use of my season pass I attended most of the home games. My seat was close enough for me to hear Red broadcasting, and with that help I was beginning to understand the fine points of baseball. Also, I was, to quote an old show biz phrase, "on the house," and with Red's most modest salary that was of paramount importance. The games became my entertainment and my escape from the confinement of the one-room apartment. The three sportswriters in the press box and Red's engineer, L. J. Barnes, became friendly acquaintances. MacPhail would often pass by and nod or give a greeting on his way for a conference with Red or one of the writers. I was always Mrs. Barber, and he was certainly always Mr. MacPhail. It was many years later when we had a home on Key Biscayne and he and his second wife Jean came there to spend their winters that we became Larry and Lylah.

At the time there were two afternoon papers in Cincinnati. Frank Y. Grayson wrote for the *Times-Star*. He was a handsome gray-haired gentleman of courtly manner who viewed the passing scene with a rather detached attitude. Tom Swope, reporter for the *Post* was younger, abrupt in manner, and abrasive in print. Jack Ryder, who covered for the morning *Enquirer*, which was the prestige paper in town, was the oldest of the writers. He considered himself dean of the press box and ruled it with an autocratic hand. Ryder would appear at the park last, just in time to get the lineup, often accompanied by Lee Allen, a young man who kept a count of the pitches and labeled them balls or strikes. His real reason for being there was to keep Ryder's Coca-Colas spiked with bourbon or gin; Ryder was a switch hitter. (Allen later became historian for the Baseball Hall of Fame in Cooperstown, New York.)

I still remember the afternoon in 1934 when things got out of hand. MacPhail had bought Tony Freitas, a young pitcher, from a minor league club, and Freitas was making his debut with the Reds.

It was a hot summer's day, and the game went into extra innings. Freitas, who pitched very well, was taken out for a pinch hitter. The relief pitcher lost the game in the next inning. During the long hot afternoon Ryder had kept himself refreshed with his reinforced Coca-Colas, and he missed the pitching substitution. Grayson and Swope tried to straighten Ryder out, but he would have no part of their help. His copy went into the paper, reporting that Freitas was knocked out of the game and was the losing pitcher. Ryder added that the rookie was "MacPhail's new lemon."

MacPhail was livid; he raged at everyone except Jack Ryder. He even blamed Red for letting his engineer get Ryder drunk. All the engineer had done was accept one of Lee Allen's Coca-Colas. To my knowledge no one ever said a word to Ryder, who continued to go his beaming-bourbon ways. No one, including MacPhail himself, dared antagonize the tyrant of the *Enquirer*.

In the fall of 1935, shortly before the close of Red's second season with the ball club, we received an informal written invitation from MacPhail saying he had been fishing in Michigan, had caught a lot of pike, and was having a fish fry for a "small group of friends" at the Netherlands Plaza, Cincinnati's new, very elegant hotel. After supper the guests would listen to the radio report of the Maxie Baer–Joe Louis fight. It was MacPhail at his most charming, and we were excited to be included. When we arrived we found out that the small group included the press, the top officials of the ball club, their wives, and us, perhaps thirty people in all. The party was in a private dining room, and the cocktail hour was in full swing. There were professional musicians and a bar offering fancy drinks whose names we had never even heard. Nothing in Gainesville, Florida, had prepared us for such splendor. We drank it all in, including the planter's punches decorated with tiny Japanese parasols. When dinner was announced and the folding doors were opened there was the table, with beautiful flowers and ice sculptures, which I had never seen before. The pike was there all right, but was only one of a number of courses, all befitting the setting. We dined, listened to the fight, said our "thank-you's," and rode the streetcar home.

I was so full of the evening that I could hardly wait for the next day to share the grandeur with my friend Mrs. Clendenning in the apartment next door. She listened and then asked very quietly, "Have you read the afternoon paper?" MacPhail had stayed late and, in the small hours, taken the elevator for the ride to the basement and his car. In the elevator he had gotten into an argument with two occupants, who turned out to be house detectives. They had given him a pretty thorough going-over, and left him with a black eye as a souvenir of the occasion.

I was learning that there were two Larry MacPhails: the sensitive, generous man of the world and the brawling, unreasonable fighter. It was the next summer that I had my poignant encounter with the "good" MacPhail. I had lost a premature baby; it was my second disappointing pregnancy, and I was crushed. At Red's pleading I finally made myself go to a ballgame. I was sitting in my accustomed seat next to the radio box and was alone. MacPhail came by and sat down beside me. He told me he was sorry about the baby, but there would be another time, that I had a good husband, on his way to a fine career, and that I must stop grieving and be a loving wife. Then he told me about the time Mrs. MacPhail had a stillborn, very premature baby. They were living in Nashville, and she had wanted the baby buried back in Ohio, I think it was, in her family plot. He had put the little fetus in a shoe box and driven all night to carry out her wishes. He shook me back into life. I stopped feeling sorry for myself. His words were badly needed and I cannot forget his caring kindness.

I did not actually see an opening day game until 1936. I stayed in the apartment the first time to hear Red's broadcast. On the second opening day I was in Riverside Hospital in Jacksonville. I had become ill while the Reds were in spring training in Tampa, and when the team started north, Red went with them. I stayed in Tampa with Aunt Ouida. I had pernicious nausea of pregnancy, and as my condition worsened Aunt Ouida drove me from Tampa to Jacksonville to my old hospital, where I lost the baby and began to learn that my husband's professional engagements came first.

In September, 1937, when our daughter Sarah was born, the new father brought us home from the hospital mid-morning and left at noon for Notre Dame and the first football game of the fall. From there he was to go to New York to broadcast the World Series. We had engaged a practical nurse to take care of the baby, and everything should have gone well. For two days it did, but then I discovered one of Sarah's little dresses in the garbage can with a brown stain down its front. The nurse had been giving my baby paregoric to keep her quiet. She went quickly, by invitation, and I soon discovered that I had a sick baby. She wouldn't or couldn't finish her bottle, and she cried both from hunger and pain. When I called the pediatrician his answer was, "Graduate nurses always make nervous mothers. Try to relax more and the baby will be more relaxed." It was terrible. What little sleeping Sarah did was mostly in the day, and I certainly got little or none at night. The World Series went to five games, and it was ten days later when Red flew back from New York and arrived home at about 2:00 A.M.

When he let himself into our apartment and made his way back to the nursery the first thing he heard was the new mother saying, in a desperate voice, "Baby, for God's sake please stop crying." By seven o'clock the next morning Red was on the telephone with the doctor, and by nine all three of us were at the hospital. X-rays quickly showed that Sarah had a pyloric spasm. Of course she cried; she was both hungry and in pain. Proper medication and the addition of some solid foods to her diet soon had her straightened out, and she quickly became a happy, healthy baby with relaxed parents.

Larry MacPhail's last year with the Reds was 1936, and the next year he was out of baseball. Warren Giles came in as general manager. He built well on MacPhail's foundation, won two pennants, won the World Series in 1940, and had consistently good teams until he left to become National League president. I remember Giles as a pleasant, quiet man. During our last two years in Cincinnati, which were also Giles' first, I was deeply involved with a new baby and had little time for either spring training or the games in the summer. My contribution was to listen to Red's broadcasts and give my impression of how they went. It was also a learning session for me. My years at St. Joseph's Academy with the nuns had not prepared me for the complexities of major league baseball.

However, there was one famous game that, quite by accident, I did see. I knew that Bob Lambert, the Episcopal minister who had baptized our daughter, was an avid fan, and I invited him and his wife Sylvia to go with me to a game. Johnny Vander Meer was the pitcher. As the game wore on I sensed the excitement in the stands. It was Bob who said, "He's going for a no-hitter." The game ended Cincinnati Reds 3, Boston Bees (as they were called then) o. And it was a no-hitter! The date was June 11, 1938. What made it so memorable was that four days later in Brooklyn, Vander Meer pitched again. The score was Cincinnati Reds 6, Brooklyn Dodgers o— the second straight no-hitter, the only time in history it has ever happened.

Red had broadcast the first no-hitter. No one broadcast the second. The three New York teams, fearing that radio would have an adverse effect on attendance, had placed a five-year ban on the broadcasting of their games. The game was played at night, the first such in the New York area. Larry MacPhail, ever the innovator, was general manager at Brooklyn by then, and he had seen to that.

The Associated Press put the double no-hitter flash on the wire, and radio station WLW immediately put the news on the air. Cincinnati went wild. Our phone, which was in Red's name, rang all night. We learned a lesson. The phone has been in my name ever since.

When Larry MacPhail returned to baseball in 1938 as general manager of the Brooklyn Dodgers, one of his first moves was to announce that when the existing contract with the Yankees and Giants forbidding all broadcasts of the games of the three New York teams terminated after that season, he was, beginning in 1939, going to put the Dodger games on the air. He signed a contract with General Mills, then the dominant sponsor of baseball games all over the country, including those at Cincinnati. General Mills signed Red to announce the games at Ebbets Field. (His subsequent contracts at Brooklyn were with advertising agencies representing sponsors until 1945, when MacPhail offered Red the Yankees radio job, and Branch Rickey, who had followed MacPhail at Brooklyn, countered with a better offer. Rickey put Red under contract to the ball club, thus beginning the policy of teams having control of who their announcers would be.)

After Powell Crosby learned that General Mills had offered Red $8,000 to announce the Brooklyn Dodgers games, he made a counter-offer of $16,000 minimum and the chance to be in charge of sports for WLW. Red thanked Crosley for the offer, but said he was going to New York. Crosley must have wondered why. I sometimes wondered, too. In 1938, $16,000 was big money. We had been in Cincinnati for five years. WLW was a powerful station with wide coverage. We had made many friends. We were putting down roots.

Mr. Crosley didn't have to wonder long. When he asked Red why he was making the change, Red replied, "For the same reasons you went broke several times before you came up with WLW. I want the chance in New York." Mr. Crosley smiled, shook hands and wished him good luck.

I didn't wonder long, either. I welcomed the news that we were going to New York. This was an exciting challenge. I was still at heart the little girl whose first words, according to my grandmother, were "go-go." Cincinnati had been kind to me, but going to New York, the big city, was exciting. And Red would be working again for MacPhail, with whom relations had been so cordial.

Our last months in Cincinnati were busy ones. Red continued doing routine studio work. In addition there were special assignments. One I remember in particular because it was interesting and great fun. One of the downtown theaters ran a combination motion picture–vaudeville program, with three, maybe four daily showings. This was the winter after Vander Meer had set his "two no-hitters back to back" record. He had become a sort of folk hero in town.

Red had broadcast the Cincinnati no-hitter, but the other game was played in Brooklyn and because of the existing radio ban in New York had not been broadcast. He was asked to do a re-creation of the crucial ninth inning following the vaudeville part of the show.

Blackstone the Magician was the current show and Red followed him. Blackstone was a charming, beautifully educated man who had been an engineer with General Electric. His wife was much younger, very pretty and friendly. She, their young son, maybe four or five years old, and a French nurse-governess traveled with the show. (The son followed in his father's footsteps. His very successful show played on Broadway during the 1979–80 season.)

It was my pleasure, during the week Red played, to attend the last show of the day and join Red and the delightful Blackstone family for a nightcap in the lounge of the lower arcade of the Netherlands Plaza Hotel. Blackstone entertained us with sleight-of-hand and card tricks, and there was much talk of life on the road traveling with a show. I was also taken backstage and shown the intricate maze of props and wires and lights that made the magic work. I can still hear Blackstone explaining, "Magic is the art of misdirection."

The show always closed with the magician standing alone against a black backdrop, beside an empty box just large enough to permit one person to lie down in it. After an elaborate pantomime demonstrating its emptiness Blackstone would place one of the girls in his troupe in the box, close it, make a few passes with his wand over the closed box, turn, and face the audience. Then, still facing the audience he would reach back, open the lid, and help out not one but six pretty girls. Of course the audience knew it was a trick, some sort of trap door probably, but they admired and enjoyed the artistic presentation. On the closing day of the show Mrs. Blackstone said to my husband, "Let's fool the magician." Everything went as usual: Blackstone faced the audience, reached back, and helped out five pretty girls. Suddenly as he took the last hand a look of surprise crossed his face—something was wrong. He turned to look at the box and there stepping out and holding his hand was Red. The audience loved it, so did the cast. Blackstone was a good sport. He joined in the merriment and the show was over.

Red's career had prospered in Cincinnati. There had been modest but steady raises. Money was easier, and we had begun to accumulate possessions, good furniture, fine china, a picture or two, our daughter's toys. The move to New York was not as simple as the one from Gainesville five years earlier. General Mills would pay all the moving expenses, but there were decisions to be made—what do we take, what do we dispose of? Finally it was all done, the moving van was loaded, and we were ready to head south to Clearwater, Florida, for spring training with our new club, the Brooklyn Dodgers.

We spent our last night in Cincinnati with Bob and Sylvia Lambert in the rectory of Calvary Church. Bob was rector of the church, and it was he who had baptized our daughter. Their invitation was most thoughtful. It gentled the farewell. We have kept in touch through the years.

NEW YORK CITY

The Brooklyn Dodgers were training in Clearwater, Florida, but Red's father was still living in Tampa. So was my aunt Ouida, and we elected to stay there. Red made the hour-long drive to Clearwater daily. Aunt Ouida had rented an apartment for us in the building where she lived with my grandmother, the Dannie of my childhood. Mother came down from Jacksonville, and we were all together, four generations of Watts women, counting Sarah. I didn't know then it was to be the only time the five of us would be together. Aunt Ouida was the first to go. She died two years later, much too young, following gall-bladder surgery. I have a picture taken then of Sarah sitting in her great-grandmother's lap. They both look quite pleased with themselves. It was a most happy spring.

When we went to spring training, Mamie, who had been our daughter's nurse and had lived with us since Sarah was less than a year old, came along. She was a small-town girl from Indiana who, like many of her friends, had gone to the city with great expectations. With little education and no special training, domestic employment became inevitable for her. She came to us straight from the Salvation Army Shelter for unmarried mothers, where her own son had been born just a few weeks before Sarah's birth. She had no choice but to place him in a foster parent program to await adoption, but she grieved for and missed her baby.

Mamie helped me with the housework, but she was primarily Sarah's nurse and such a good one. My child got the love Mamie could not give her own and thrived on her double portion. It was through sharing Mamie's pain vicariously that I first became interested in the plight of the unwed mother and later in New York did volunteer work for her cause.

Because we had Mamie with us to take care of Sarah, and Aunt Ouida nearby in case of an emergency, Red and I were able to have a little vacation by ourselves for the first time since Sarah's birth. Neither of us had been to Key West, and we both wanted to see it. We drove down the West Coast throught the small towns, almost villages, of Bradenton, Sarasota, Fort Myers (Thomas A. Edison's adopted town), and Naples. This was years before the West Coast of Florida became the overcrowded tourist area it now is. There were good roads, but no four-lane highways, and large areas of undeveloped beaches with beautiful views of the Gulf.

At Naples we picked up the western end of the Tamiami Trail which runs through the Everglades, the Indians' River of Grass, to the east coast. It was a desolate landscape, almost without evidence of human habitation. We saw an occasional Seminole dwelling, a simple platform built on stilts, its only protection from the elements a palm-leaf roof. We did pass one settlement, and perhaps an occasional hunting-fishing lodge, but mostly there were only the birds, heron and ibis, standing in the canals or in flight. The lonely land spoke to me. I felt a great sense of peace. I feel the same way about Sidney Lanier's Marshes of Glynn, outside Brunswick, Georgia.

We turned south at the eastern end of the Trail, driving through the southern tip of the Florida peninsula over a narrow bridge onto Key Largo, the largest of the Keys. Then we headed for Key West. Highway US 1 led for hours from one small sandy key to another, with the waters of the Gulf on our right and the Atlantic Ocean on our left. The road was two-lane all the way. The bridges were narrow, except for one, the Seven Mile Bridge, a marvel of twentieth-century engineering, which stretches from Marathon to Bahia Honda over an expanse of blue-green water.

We reached Key West at sunset. I remember being surprised at how small it was. We stayed at a small commercial hotel, the only one in town. We had passed a large resort-type hotel about two miles east of Key West, but it was closed. Key West was still reeling from the combined effects of the Depression and the violent hurricane which had destroyed the roadbed of the Overseas Railroad that tied Key West to the mainland. There had been a heavy loss of life.

The flavor of the town was much more Caribbean than American. Even then, there were political refugees from Cuba. Most of the old

Dannie, with her great-granddaughter Sarah Lanier Barber.

families were of English stock and had come from the Bahamas. They brought with them the Bahamian-Colonial architecture, and we enjoyed wandering around the old town and seeing the handsome two-story houses with their wide verandahs designed to catch the cooling trade winds. We ate in small Cuban restaurants and enjoyed the spicy food and the sound of the staccato Cuban Spanish. The two days were like a short trip abroad.

When we returned to Tampa it was time to pack our clothes, get in our green Lincoln Zephyr, our first automobile, say our good-byes to the family, and head for New York and the new job. With the combination of the great city and Larry MacPhail for boss, it had to be interesting and exciting and we were anxious to get going. Red and I sat in front, and Mamie had the back seat with our active year-and-a-half-old Sarah. After our lunch break I would take Sarah up front with me so that Mamie could have a short nap. She was wonderfully patient with the baby. Fortunately Sarah was no longer on a formula, with its attendant bottles, and everyone welcomed the restaurant stops. Even so it was a long trip, and we all were glad when we finally drove over the Pulaski Skyway, through the Holland Tunnel and into the late afternoon rush-hour traffic of New York City.

We had no hotel reservations. Red had just turned thirty-one the month before, and with the supreme confidence of youth he pulled into a parking place that was waiting for him in front of a drugstore. Can you imagine just finding a parking place anywhere in New York City today? Earlier that spring Red had flown up from Tampa for a planning conference with WOR, the station that was to broadcast the Brooklyn games, and had met Eugene Thomas, who was sales manager for the station. Now he went into the drugstore, phoned WOR, and asked to speak to Thomas. Fortunately he was in, and Red said, "We're here. Where do I find a two-bedroom, two-bath apartment?" The request didn't seem to faze Thomas. He simply said, "Go to the Beaux Arts. It's on 44th Street just two blocks east of Grand Central. They will have what you need." They did, including a small but adequate kitchenette and a balcony with a view of the boat traffic on the East River. By nightfall we were at home in New York City.

This morning, as I write here at home in Tallahassee over forty years later, I asked my husband, "How did you ever have the nerve?" He said quietly, "I knew New York was a big city and there would be room for us. If I hadn't had the nerve we would still be in Gainesville, Florida."

Red immediately began broadcasting the spring training exhibition games of the Dodgers from Western Union reports. This was the reason we had come to New York early. In those years major league teams barnstormed their way home, playing games with each other in towns along the way. They traveled by train in their own private cars and diner—hotel and restaurant as well as transportation. Larry MacPhail was very smart, well ahead of his times. He wanted his games to be the first heard in New York. The Giants and Yankees, in their smugness and overconfidence, felt that the broadcast of exhibition games was beneath them. They were also still smarting from being forced by MacPhail into broadcasting games at all. Consequently, by opening day of the National League season the Brooklyn games had been aired for a month with no competition, and MacPhail had already won many of his loyal listening fans.

My immediate assignment was to find a house in the suburbs for the family. That first year in New York there were three sponsors for the broadcast of the games: Wheaties, Mobil Oil and Mobil Gas, and Ivory Soap. Red knew that Hal James, the young agency contact-man for Ivory Soap, had lived in Westchester County, and he enlisted his help. Hal's wife had grown up in Scarsdale. She put us in touch with Julia Braccallelo, a realtor friend of hers, who quickly found us a small house to rent, just two blocks from the commuting station, and we became residents of Scarsdale. Hal James, who had been so helpful in getting us settled, later became a successful producer on Broadway. He was co-producer of *Man of La Mancha*, a beautiful play which enjoyed a long run.

During the several weeks we lived at the Beaux Arts while I was house-hunting and then waiting for our furniture to come from Cincinnati I commuted to prepare the house for occupancy. I was also busy getting acquainted with New York, my new hometown. Evenings both Red and I were free, and Cliff Samuelson, the agency man who represented General Mills and Wheaties, began showing us the town. We were avid students and had great fun. Our first big treat was being taken to La Crémaillère, a small French restaurant on East 62nd Street. It occupied two floors of an old brownstone house between Fifth and Madison Avenues. Cliff insisted on ordering for us, which was just as well. Certainly neither one of us knew our way around a menu in French. When the first course arrived we were aghast. Snails in their shells—yes, we had seen them before, but only in gardens in Florida, where they were slimy pests. Fortified by my pre-dinner drink I gingerly tasted them; they were delicious, of course. La Crémaillère became our favorite restaurant, and afterwards we dined there on our wedding anniversary each March 28 when we were not in Florida for spring training, on birthdays, whenever our parents visited, to celebrate a raise or a new job— things very special. Over the years we became friends with Monsieur Antoine Gilly, who was chef and owner of La Crémaillère. When the row of old brownstones was razed to build the modern Carlton House, Monsieur Gilly opened La Crémaillère à la Campagne in Banksville, New York, near his country home. It became an internationally famous restaurant, and we went there often when we were living in Westchester County, but it was never quite the same as the one in the little brownstone on East 62nd Street. When Antoine retired, he went back to his beloved France. So far as I know he is still living in Nice.

Cliff Samuelson also introduced us to Mama Leone's on West 48th Street. It was quite different from our little quiet, reserved French restaurant of a few nights before. Leone's was big, very Italian in decor and exuberance, and filled with friendly visiting people from the world of the theater and sports. Everybody seemed to know everybody else and to be happy about it. That first night we arrived late and left very much later. We waded into the antipasto, the best, the most elaborate I've ever had anywhere, including the finest restaurants in Italy. We went through the alphabet from antipasto to zabaglione. Cliff ordered French 75's for after-dinner drinks. By this time it was past midnight and the restaurant was almost empty. Gene Leone came over, introduced himself, and sat down. He was most cordial, and the four of us began visiting. Red mentioned that his best man at our wedding was Frank DeGaetani, an Italian from New York. "I know him well," said Gene, "we grew up on the same block in Little Italy."

If it begins to sound as though we spent most of our time eating, well, we did enjoy it. Cincinnati had good restaurants when we lived there, but it had been settled largely by German and Irish immigrants, and the food tended to be a bit heavy and not of great variety. New York was a gourmet's delight. We did take time for a couple of Broadway shows and a performance of the New York Philharmonic

Red, with his father and Sarah.

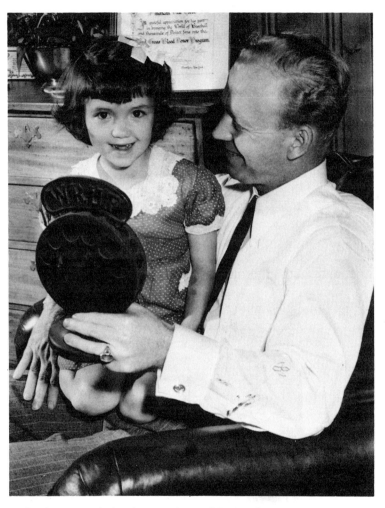

Sarah—note missing front teeth—and Red at first microphone he ever spoke into, at Gainesville.

Orchestra. As soon as we could afford it I bought a season ticket to the Philharmonic, and during the twenty-eight years that we lived in New York I was a faithful member of the audience at the Odd Friday afternoon concerts. Everything was new and wonderful. When the house in Scarsdale was finally ready for us to move into, it was with a twinge of regret that I left the Beaux Arts.

Several of my college friends had preceded me to New York. My roommate Virginia Bisant, the music major with the beautiful voice, was hostess in the very popular Alice Foote McDougall tearoom. Ruth Miller, tall, slender, and good-looking, modelled tea gowns (what has become of them?) for Bergdorf Goodman. Beth Price was lucky. Dr. Myrtle McGraw, under whom Beth had taken a course in child psychology at Florida State College for Women, had gone to Columbia University to do research on the phenomenon of identical twins, under Dr. Fred Tilney at the Neurological Institute of Columbia Medical Center. Beth and Annie Houstoun, another of Dr. McGraw's students, became her assistants. Other friends went to work at Macy's department store.

I don't remember how Martha Jones, one of my Theta sisters, and I found each other, but there she was, living in Scarsdale with her husband, Frank Cavallon, an assistant manager in the furniture department at Macy's. Their son Michael was nine months older than Sarah and their daughter Mary nine months younger.

I had friends, Sarah had playmates, and Red was climbing rapidly in his profession.

Our first spring training in Florida after we moved to New York, in 1940, saw the Brooklyn ball club quartered in the old Belleview Biltmore Hotel in Belleair, a small resort town near Clearwater. It was a typical MacPhail choice, high-class and expensive but in some ways a relic of the past. Our suite was spotless and comfortable. There was plenty of room for the three of us, but the bathroom plumbing certainly was not current 1940. There was a big tub on claw feet, and the water tank for the toilet was suspended on the wall, close to the ceiling, with its chain and handle hanging within arm's reach. The clientele was mostly elderly retired industrialists and professionals and their wives from the Eastern Seaboard and the Middle West. There was the usual smattering of ancient dowagers, and a few younger couples with their children on spring vacation.

Judge Kennesaw Mountain Landis, the first commissioner of baseball, was staying at the hotel. He was a handsome, courtly gentleman with an imposing shock of white hair. Judge Landis had been brought into baseball after the notorious Chicago White Sox scandal. Eight players had been involved in taking money from gamblers to throw certain games in the 1919 World Series with Cincinnati. Baseball at that time had no commissioner. It was run by a three-man committee. The owners brought in Landis, a federal judge, to save their most valuable asset, the belief of the public in the integrity of baseball. Landis came in with absolute authority. Mr. and Mrs. Ford C. Frick—he was then president of the National League— were also staying at the Belleview Biltmore. Ford Frick was to become the third commissioner of baseball, succeeding Happy Chandler, who resigned from the U.S. Senate to become commissioner upon the death of Judge Landis.

Children were allowed in the main dining room only for breakfast. By necessity Sarah and I ate our luncheon in the children's dining room, and I would take her back there around six o'clock for her light supper. I was the only adult in the children's dining room who wasn't either a nanny or a mamselle. To me it somehow seemed a sad place. The nurses were, for the most part, bored and made little effort to amuse the children. Fortunately the children were absorbed in their own projects. I remember one episode in particular. A golf tournament was in progress among the guests of the hotel. The mother of two of the young people, a boy and a girl, had been eliminated in the morning's final round. She came into the dining room appearing downcast and, I sensed, looking for sympathy. The children did not even look up from their plates. The nurse finally said, "Children, your mother lost her game. Tell her you are sorry." They turned, said, "Sorry, Mother," and resumed eating. Somehow, high society didn't seem so happy.

MacPhail, with his loud voice and explosive temper, must have been a trial for the hotel staff. At any rate, neither he nor the hotel seemed too pleased with the arrangement, and the next two years he took the club to Havana. The Dodgers never did return to Clearwater. After World War II the team, under Branch Rickey, went to Daytona Beach in 1946, Cuba in 1947, the Dominican Republic in 1948, and then to Dodgertown at Vero Beach.

In 1941 the Dodgers beat the Braves in Boston to clinch their first pennant in twenty-one years. Brooklyn went wild. It was my first realization of how powerful, even frightening, mass hysteria, be it happy or angry, can become. At that time WOR carried the Brooklyn games and John Hayes, who was an executive at the station, invited me to come in from Scarsdale, where we were then living, and go with him to Grand Central Station to see the excitement when the team came in from Boston. There was excitement for sure. By the time we arrived the upper level was a solid mass of screaming, happy fans. The closest our group could get was on the mezzanine. It was close enough. We had an unencumbered view of the goings-on below but were safe from the milling of the crowd. I am only five feet tall and prone to claustrophobia.

Finally the players arrived at the gate where Red stood with a microphone, trying for a word or two as they went by. The police cleared a path for them through the people. It wasn't easy. When Leo Durocher, the manager, and the last player came through and the gates were closed, the fans turned their attention to the "voice" of the Dodgers. Red's thick, curly red hair became a target. They began literally tearing at it for souvenirs. I watched, and my fright grew. Suppose their happy mood changed and they became mean? What chance would he have, jammed in among them? Fortunately the crowd began to disperse, and to my relief he soon joined us.

But the reception at Grand Central is only a part of the story. MacPhail had chosen to go to 125th Street to join his ball club when the train stopped there, as was customary. Branch Rickey showed up at the platform to take another train west. He was then general manager of the St. Louis Cardinals, and the two teams had battled each other all summer for the pennant. Rickey's team had lost out that very day.

The two men waited. But what they didn't know was that Durocher, knowing that his players were anxious to avoid the crowd at Grand Central and were planning to get off at 125th Street, had told the conductor not to stop the train. He didn't. The train roared by. There stood MacPhail in anger and embarrassment, and, to make it worse, with Rickey to witness his humiliation. MacPhail fired Durocher that night. But on second thought, and cooling off, he rehired him the next morning.

The Yankees won the World Series in five games. That was the year Mickey Owen dropped the third strike in the fourth game. Everything happened to the Dodgers.

THE MacPHAIL I KNEW

The immediate impact of the Japanese attack on Pearl Harbor and America's entry into World War II was not overly crippling insofar as the effect on playing personnel of the major league baseball teams was concerned. It was not until the 1943 season that many of the game's leading players were absent in the armed forces. In the last ten days of the 1942 pennant race, MacPhail's final season as general manager, Brooklyn was overtaken by the St. Louis Cardinals and finished out of the running.

The United States was now deeply committed to the war effort. MacPhail had been a young officer, a captain, in World War I. Even then he was involved in a typically flamboyant adventure—a plot to kidnap the Kaiser. So it was no surprise when he resigned at Brooklyn and joined General George C. Marshall's staff as a lieutenant colonel.

That ended my husband's professional relationship with MacPhail, but, as I write, I am struck by how often he kept coming back into our lives. After the war, in 1947, Branch Rickey took the Dodgers to Havana for spring training. He had broken major league baseball's unwritten bar against black players by signing Jackie Robinson to a contract. Because of the South's segregation laws the team could not train there with Robinson in camp.

By this time Red was also director of sports at CBS and had gone to Miami a week ahead for a series of golf broadcasts. Sarah and I were to join him later for the flight to Havana. She was by then ten years old, and it was not so easy to take her out of school for long absences. On the train trip down she became ill. By the time we reached Miami it was obvious that she had a high fever and was quite sick. Her father and I held a quick conference on the station platform. It was almost time for the short flight to Havana, where we would be for some three or four weeks; since there were good doctors available there, it made sense to continue and get her settled.

It was good thinking, but it didn't quite work out. When we were within sight of Havana the plane ran into a quick tropical storm. We could see the waves going over the Malecón, the seawall that protects the city. The pilot could not land, and turned back to Key West and the shelter of the Naval Air Station. Since the plane had been cleared for Cuba, the passengers were not allowed to get off. We sat for several dark hours in the heat, without any air conditioning, and with a sick child. Finally the storm was over, and we flew back to Havana.

By the time we cleared customs and got to the hotel it was well past midnight. The desk clerk could not, or would not, find our room reservation made by the ball club. Mr. Rickey and Harold Parrott, the road secretary whose job it was to take care of such matters, were at a press relations banquet. There was nothing to do but wait in the lobby. I settled Sarah on a bench, with her head in my lap.

Suddenly and most surprisingly there appeared Larry MacPhail. He was back in baseball as president of the New York Yankees and co-owner with Dan Topping and Del Webb. They had brought the Yankees to Havana for a series of exhibition games with the Dodgers. He saw the three of us and came over. I suppose we looked pretty forlorn because he said, "What's the matter?" When Red explained he turned to Arthur Patterson, his press relations man, and said, "Give them the key to your room and bunk with one of the writers." He also sent Dr. Mal Stevens, the Yankees' physician, to check on Sarah. To me that night MacPhail was guardian angel and Santa Claus all in one.

When MacPhail first took charge of the Yankees in 1945 he had sent for Red and offered him the broadcasting assignment and a three-year contract for $100,000. This was long before the era of astronomical fees, and it was a lot of money then. Red was tempted, but he finally decided to stay at Brooklyn. When Red made his decision, MacPhail was disappointed. Yet he smiled, shook hands, and said, "My offer didn't hurt you with Rickey, did it?"

I have often wondered how different my life might have been had

Larry MacPhail and friend.

Red taken up MacPhail's offer of a three-year contract for $100,000. Remember, this was in the days of radio only. Television was several years in the future. I was amazed. Had Red accepted MacPhail's offer I am sure life would have been exciting. How could it have been otherwise, with MacPhail running the show? His offer was to come to Yankee Stadium for the seasons of 1946, 1947, and 1948. Branch Rickey countered with an offer of $105,000 for the same three years. My husband elected to remain at Brooklyn with the Dodgers and Rickey. Maybe the explosive years with MacPhail had been enough.

Some twenty years later when we bought a house on Key Biscayne, we were settled as permanent residents on the island before we found out that Larry and Jean, his second wife, and young Jeanie, their teenage daughter, were spending the winters there. Red was busy with broadcasting and speaking engagements and writing a weekly column for the Miami *Herald*. I was frequently alone, and the MacPhails helped me fill many long hours. They took me to football games and invited me to suppers. Larry would often cook fresh fish that he had caught. Most of the time it was very pleasant, but if I sensed an air of tension or found that he had a headstart on the cocktail hour, I would remember my husband saying that when MacPhail started drinking in the press room after ball games, he would find he had business elsewhere and leave. I would follow his advice and go home before the storm broke.

The MacPhails' young daughter Jeanie was a student at Carrollton Convent, the fine prep school in Coconut Grove run by the Mesdames of the Sacred Heart, a French order of nuns. One Christmas Larry sent the nuns a case of French champagne for a season's gift. I'm sure the sister headmistress must have been pleased and a little amused as she saw it sitting among the more customary pots of red poinsettias.

Key Biscayne, at the time we were all living there, was still a small island settlement. It had originally been a coconut plantation and many of the trees were still standing. Construction of the Rickenbacker Causeway (built after World War II and named for World War I hero Eddie Rickenbacker) had tied the island to the mainland and opened it up to the developers. The Mackle brothers had built a number of small houses and there were a few ocean-front motels, but the big boom of large hotels and expensive private homes was still to come.

The relatively small number of Episcopalians on the island were holding Sunday services in a small, one-room wooden building which had originally been a dormitory for migrant workers on the coconut plantation. The bishop had sent Richard Maholm as vicar to establish a mission. By the time we arrived in 1965 the congregation had grown and plans were afoot for buying land and building a church. Father Maholm asked Red to serve on a three-member committee along with Wyly Billing, chairman, and Harold Abbott, charged with raising the necessary money.

Fundraising is hard business, and publicity is the name of the game. Red appealed to his friend Larry. Would he preach at a Sunday service at the little dormitory building? Red hoped the news that MacPhail was to be in the pulpit would engender interest. It did. MacPhail in the pulpit was news, and the Miami *Herald* gave it coverage. Larry spoke well. His bearing was decorous, and in his choir vestments he looked, to borrow a current phrase, quite "born again."

Red had one more favor to ask. Would Larry give a fundraising cocktail party at Island House? The MacPhails had recently moved into the brand-new, very expensive condominium building on the ocean. It was filled with "fat cats," very wealthy retired people who wintered there. Larry agreed, and everyone from Bishop James Duncan down was invited. They all knew what to expect, but they came. The party was MacPhail at his best. The house club room was filled with flowers, there were strolling musicians, the hors d'oeuvres were plentiful and good, and the liquid refreshment flowed freely. At intervals Larry would disappear into a room down the hall with one of the "fat cats" in tow. He would soon be back, grinning, with a pledge in hand. The party was a great success. Later when MacPhail gave his contribution to Wyly Billing he handed over a $1,000 check, saying, "It's my stud fee for one of my thoroughbred stallions." Harold Abbott, that most proper of Englishmen, gave a small gasp, smiled, and accepted the check.

Larry MacPhail died in his eighty-fifth year in a Miami nursing home. It was not fitting; he should have gone in the heat of battle.

The mystery of Larry MacPhail's different personalities—the towering rage finding release in physical contact, often against the helpless, and the instant generous response to another's hurt or need—I saw at first hand. The good MacPhail and the bad Mac-Phail—I loved them both.

THE WAR YEARS

When Branch Rickey came to Brooklyn as general manager of the ball club in the fall of 1942 he was sixty-one years old. He and Mrs. Rickey took an apartment in Bronxville near the house we had built in Scarsdale, and he invited Red and me to come for luncheon. It was my first contact with Mr. Rickey. I met a heavy-set, stocky man with brown hair streaked with gray. His alert dark eyes looked out from under bushy brown eyebrows. I later learned that he always wore bow ties, never wore a watch, and often didn't carry any money. His expensive, custom-made suits gave the appearance of rumpled, indifferent grooming. He was not interested in the ordinary routines of life.

When he traveled on short notice, as he often did, Mrs. Rickey always packed his grips. He would phone her from the office, saying, "Jane, I'm making a speech at a dinner in Toledo [or Seattle, or Denver]. Pack my tuxedo." One of my favorite stories about the two of them is the time he began dressing for a dinner. The dinner jacket was there all right, but no pants. Fortunately the tablecloth and speaker's lectern hid his brown traveling trousers. After dinner he sent Mrs. Rickey a telegram: "Jane, I know you wear the pants, but where are they?"

Later in their friendship Mr. Rickey told Red why I had been invited to that first luncheon. "Walter [Mr. Rickey never called my husband by his nickname], the most important person in a man's life is his wife. When I enter into a professional relationship with a man I must know about his wife. When a young ballplayer begins, suddenly, to play below his established ability I ask his manager why. If he doesn't know I ask the trainer, for that is a very close relationship. If the trainer doesn't know I send for the player's wife. I explain that her well-being depends on her husband's performance. Then I get the story."

The deep love between Mr. and Mrs. Rickey was beautiful to

watch and be allowed to share. In the first years of their married life there were no children. The Rickeys then had in rapid succession a girl, Branch, Jr., and four more girls. Young Branch was called, in the family, simply Boy. Mrs. Rickey laughingly told me that once when she was interviewing someone for the job of laundress and showed her the hamper of children's clothing, the applicant looked in amazement and said, "Mrs. Rickey, is you Catholic or careless?"

When I went to the ball games I was privileged to sit in the president's box with Mrs. Rickey and her unmarried sister Miss Moulton, who lived with them. During the course of the years I came to know the Rickey daughters and their children. Branch, Jr.'s wife Mary was often present at games. Sometimes I took our daughter Sarah with me on Sunday afternoons. Mrs. Rickey was kind and wise. She taught me a lot about coping with the frustration of having to share much of my husband's time with the demands of his successful career. I needed her friendly, concerned reassurance. She told me of the difficulties of the years when the children were young. Once she said, "When the children are small their troubles are small. When they are grown their troubles are big." I didn't believe her then; I was too involved in sore throats and mumps and broken bones. (Sarah waited until she had been teaching second grade for several years in the heart of Harlem to have measles.) Mrs. Rickey, of course, was right.

Mr. Rickey's years as general manager of the Dodgers presented him with serious problems. The war was on. Many of the best players were being drafted. Others had volunteered for military service following Pearl Harbor. There were severe travel restrictions, and gasoline was rationed. The trains were crowded with troops on the move. German submarines were offshore in the Atlantic preying on the vessels carrying men, oil, and munitions to our allies in Europe. The bright lights of the city made them easier targets for the U-boats, and New York soon went under a dim-out. The Statue of Liberty's light went off and remained so for the duration. Times Square's neon signs were dimmed, and Coney Island went dark. Night ball games at the Polo Grounds and Ebbets Field were rescheduled (Yankee Stadium was still without lights). Games could be started in the late afternoon, but they had to be over within one hour of sunset.

The travel restrictions had made spring training in the South impossible. Mr. Rickey, nothing if not resourceful, was fortunate enough to secure the use of the enclosed and heated field house at West Point when it was not being used by the cadets. The ball club and the press were housed at Bear Mountain Inn, five miles south on the Hudson River. John Martin, who managed the inn for the New York State Parks Department, was an avid sports fan and a friend of many people in the world of baseball and football. He was a most gracious and helpful host. The club trained at Bear Mountain in the war years of 1943–45.

Red and I were seldom there. Sarah was by then in school, and, although we lived only a short drive up the Hudson to West Point, what little gas we were allotted went mainly to the carpool for Sarah's transportation. Then, too, Red was working full-time from the end of the baseball season in the fall to opening day in the spring as volunteer chairman of fundraising for the Red Cross, first in 1943–44 in Brooklyn, and again in 1944–45 in both Brooklyn and Manhattan. The 1944–45 campaign raised some $20 million.

Red's first contact with the Red Cross had come on opening day in 1942. Walter Ripperger, a volunteer worker for the Brooklyn chapter, had come to the broadcasting booth and asked if Red would make an appeal for blood donors to supply needed blood for the armed forces. At the time there was a strong taboo against the use of the word "blood" on the air. For instance, it could not be used to describe the result of a blow to the nose or eye of a participant in a prize fight. For permission to make the appeal my husband took Ripperger to MacPhail, who at the time was still general manager at Brooklyn. MacPhail's reply was short and to the point. "Hell," he said, "there's a war on." Until the end of the war Red made his daily appeals for blood and the public responded. How time changes our mores. That was 1942–45. Several years ago, in 1980, I listened to and watched the televising of the second game of the World Series and I was shocked and disgusted. Repeatedly there were reports on the condition of third baseman George Brett's hemorrhoids.

We spent occasional weekends at Bear Mountain, and I remember them most warmly. In the spring of 1945 when the war was drawing to a close and it seemed likely that that would be the Dodgers' last time for training at Bear Mountain, Mr. Rickey and the Dodgers gave a dinner in honor of John Martin. It was a grand occasion. John and Marie, his warm, fun-loving wife, and their children had become close personal friends. At the end of the dinner Mr. Rickey gave a most moving, sincere speech of appreciation (he was a masterful after-dinner speaker), and presented John with a gold lifetime pass to Ebbets Field. Marie died, tragically, a short time afterward. She was, I think, in her early forties. She went into the hospital for minor nose or throat surgery, I believe it was, and died under the anesthetic before the surgery had begun. John died a few years later, while still in his prime.

Those war years were hard but challenging. Pearl Harbor had shocked and aroused the general public. Between the draft and enlistments there were few people who did not have at least one close relative in the armed services. My brother Mat, who was a thirty-three-year-old bachelor, received his greetings immediately and went into the Army Air Corps. Red's brother Billy, who was seven years younger and married, volunteered but failed the physical examination because of an abdominal hernia. With a typical, impulsive Billy gesture, he paid to have the hernia repaired, presented himself again, and was accepted by the Army. After going through officer's training school, he saw considerable combat duty in Europe. Although he was married, Billy had no children, and when hostilities ended he was not among the service personnel to be returned home early. Instead, he was sent with the army of occupation to Austria, where he was placed in charge of the officers' club in Linz. For once the Army had the right man in the right job. He thoroughly enjoyed it, as, I'm sure, did his fellow officers.

On the home front "make do" became the rule. Gasoline was rationed; so were meat and sugar. A few people cheated and dealt on the black market, but most were honest; certainly our friends were. We walked everywhere. Car pools were formed to take husbands to the commuting station for the trains that carried them into New York. Because Red and the ball games were on a different schedule from the other men he rode his bicycle the two miles to the station. For the few social evenings we enjoyed, walking shoes and, on snowy evenings, snow boots and ski pants became the "in" fashions.

As for food rationing, there is one incident I remember well. It concerns the rationing of meat and the family weakness for animals. At the time we had two pets, an English bull called, because of a certain resemblance in appearance and temperament, Queen Victoria, and a Siamese cat who, since Red shared a home with my mother, our daughter, and me, was known as Onli Son. They were most of the time good friends. Since what meat brought into the house was precious, and went for the most part to our young daughter, it was carefully guarded. Groceries were ordered by phone and delivered by the grocery truck. I had cautioned the driver, if I were not in the kitchen, to put anything enticing to the cat in the refrigerator rather than on the counter in easy reach. I was surprised and pained when one morning I walked into the kitchen and found the priceless pound of bacon—what was left of it—not in the refrigerator, but on top of it, where the prize had been discovered by Onli Son who like all Siamese was an excellent climber and jumper. He apparently had made it from the stove to the top of the refrigerator. With the aid of teeth and claws, he had gotten the package open and its contents were being devoured by a happy cat. Some slices had made their way to the floor where they were discovered by Vickie, who was also feasting. Not only was most of the meat gone but the wonderful bacon fat that I, being a true child of the South, used to give some flavor to our mainly vegetarian diet was lost.

Few people will agree with me but, having spent most of my lifetime in the company of cats, I am convinced that Onli Son, in a rare burst of generosity, had tossed a few pieces to his friend. He was much too smart to have such a thing happen by accident.

Vickie, the English bull who got the precious bacon, was the dog we had bought as a puppy when we first came to Scarsdale to live. It was not too many years since the Lindbergh kidnapping and there had been several other abductions of children. Because my husband's name and voice had become well known, we were apprehensive for our child's safety. Vickie had been bought to be her companion and watch dog. Sarah was delighted with the puppy and a bed was bought for Vickie and placed in Sarah's bedroom. We assumed that things had gone well the first night but the second bedtime, Sarah, to our surprise, protested that she did not want Vickie with her. "Why?" we asked. "Because she snores and keeps me awake." Vickie spent the rest of her nights with us sleeping in the kitchen.

Domestic helpers all but disappeared. They were doing their "war bit" in the munitions and clothing factories supplying the materials needed for the military. The Mamie of Sarah's infancy and early childhood had long since gone back to Indiana. Our home was large, and I am a compulsively neat housekeeper, a trait my mother passed on to me. Mother, who was then living with us, was the same young bride of whom my father had cried, "Mama, she doesn't know how to cook." She still had not found her way to the kitchen.

Because of its strategic location near New York and Boston, the two great ports of embarkation for military personnel going to and returning from the European theater of war, our home became a sort of way-station for relatives and friends in the service. There were many house-guests paying visits of uncertain duration, and I was kept busy.

My brother Mat passed his last weeks in training, before being shipped to England, in a factory on Long Island which manufactured the P47 Thunderbolt, the great fighter plane of World War II. He spent most of his free time with us. Oscar Bisant, the brother of my college roommate, who was by then a major, was our guest for a night. He had just finished intensive training in jungle warfare and was on his way to re-assignment.

Red's brother Billy was with us for a last leave before reporting to his port of embarkation in Massachusetts. Red's sister Virginia came up from Washington. When Lieutenant Billy arrived he also brought

The house on Sherbrooke Road, Scarsdale, New York—*photo by Jacob Lofman.*

his captain and the captain's wife. I was flabbergasted. Where was I going to sleep all these people? Of course we managed, but it took some figuring. Sarah slept with her grandmother. Virginia curled up in Sarah's youth bed. The captain and his wife drew the day-bed in the library, and Billy, who was quite tall, did as best he could with the couch in the living room.

It didn't make much difference anyway. Mother and Sarah retired early. The captain and his wife followed a little later. The family, the four of us, stayed up late, never voicing our fear but knowing full well this might be the last time we would all be together. There wasn't much time for sleep. Five o'clock and a quick breakfast of coffee and toast came soon. We left Mother and Sarah still sleeping. When the six of us got in the car it was still dark, and the snow was beginning to come down in big wet globs. They got bigger and bigger, and by the time daylight finally came the road was almost impassable. To make matters more difficult, as we neared Stamford the car burned out a bearing. We made it slowly to the railroad station and put Billy and the captain on a train to Boston. Virginia and the captain's wife headed by rail for New York. Red and I slowly made our way, in a disabled car and a worsening storm, back to Scarsdale. It was late in the afternoon when we finally arrived. There would be three long, anxious years before we saw Billy again.

Memory is so selective. As I write about these war years I recall vividly my sense of personal isolation. The house we had built in Scarsdale, with pride and such a sense of achievement, and moved into the January after Pearl Harbor, sat on top of a hill in its own heavily wooded two acres. There was not a neighbor within sight. Our small daughter had no companions within walking distance. Her afternoons and weekends were lonely. Our social contacts with friends were limited by the restrictions of the times. The concern and fear for the safety and life of our two brothers engaged in combat in Europe was ever present. I was fortunate; my husband was with me. But it was like living on borrowed time, waiting for the always possible greetings from Uncle Sam and his draft board.

Because of his two jobs (the Red Cross chairmanship and the broadcasts of the area baseball and football games), Red's working days were long and for the most part seven days a week. The company that manufactured Old Gold cigarettes had bought the baseball rights in 1941. Later Old Gold expanded its radio advertising coverage to include a weekly variety-musical show. Red became combination master of ceremonies and commercial announcer. There was an eight o'clock show with an eleven o'clock repeat to the West Coast, which meant taking a commuting train home after midnight. Like all entertainment at the time, the show was geared to the war effort. There were big name bands with guest artists, and always a spot featuring a service man, with some sort of surprise for him.

Occasionally Mother would take care of Sarah for me, and after fixing them a light supper I would ride the train into town for the show. I recall one service man's surprise that really backfired. Some bright young agency man conceived the idea of bringing the service man's mother to New York and having her join him on stage from the wings. He greeted her appearance with stony silence. It seemed they had been estranged and had not seen each other for several years. She had accepted, hoping I suppose for a reconciliation, but he would have no part of it. That was the last "surprise" of so personal a nature.

Otherwise, the show was a great success. Among others, I recall seeing and hearing the bands of Sammy Kaye, Frankie Carle, and Woody Herman. Alec Templeton, Georgie Jessel, Jackie Gleason, and many others made guest appearances. After the early show we would all—producer, agency personnel, announcer, sometimes guest artist, and assorted wives—go together for dinner at some nearby restaurant while we waited for the repeat show. I loved those evenings. They were a welcome break from the lonely evenings in the country.

There were other "evenings in town," such as the big Red Cross fundraising rally in Madison Square Garden in early March of 1945. The Garden was packed to the rafters. The great, near-great, and journeymen from the world of the performing arts were there to entertain the crowd. Helen Hayes and Mrs. Franklin Delano Roosevelt were the honored guests.

In the years that I lived, because of my husband's career, in their world I found the artists most responsive to worthwhile appeals for help. They gave freely of their time and talent. While Red was raising money for the Red Cross he counted heavily on the stars of the legitimate theater. Gertrude Lawrence, the great star of *Lady in the Dark*, was his chairwoman in charge of raising money from the people of the stage. She was industrious and successful, but Red could never teach her to keep books. She just didn't think it was important. At an afternoon rally in Brooklyn I heard the very young, slender Frank Sinatra sing, and overheard someone ask, "Who is the young boy with the golden voice?" He was almost unknown at the time.

Another and all too vivid war memory has to do with the time Red asked me to make a special trip into town for dinner. "Meet me at the Chambord," he said. I was surprised. It was then one of the best-known restaurants in the city, famous for its fine food. We had often spoken of trying it but had heard it was frightfully expensive and figured we had better save it for a very special occasion. I thought, "Perhaps he has a new program." Well, it was expensive, and the food was excellent. The champagne, a real treat, was delicious. When the meal was finished and it was time to leave I asked, "Why the celebration?" He told me, "I got my greetings from the draft board this morning telling me I had been reclassified I-A and to hold myself ready for drafting and induction into the armed forces." The champagne went flat with a bang. I could feel the tears, but I had been too well trained by my Watts women ancestors to make a scene in public. I think my husband counted on that. A few weeks later my fears were dissipated when General Hershey issued a directive that no more fathers or men over a certain age were to be inducted. Red was thirty-six and a father. I was grateful and felt myself lucky.

My family and I shared a happy and maturing experience as a result of the tight domestic situation which prevailed in those war years. I had been without any household help for a long time when I heard through a friend that the Methodist Church had been approached by the federal government to sponsor a program bringing Japanese from the internment camps on the West Coast to the East Coast for rehabilitation and jobs. The war in Europe was coming toward its end, and some of the hysteria that followed the attack on Hawaii had abated. People were beginning to realize that a grave injustice had been done many loyal Japanese immigrants and countless Nisei and that there should be some effort to make amends.

I contacted the agency and explained my need. I was told they would make some inquiries and be back in touch with me later in the day. A second call told me to expect a gentleman and his wife on a certain train the next morning, that he had been an owner of a chain of Japanese-type inns on the West Coast before the war, that his wife did not speak or understand English, and that he would interpret for her. They had two daughters and were interested in finding a place for them to live outside the barracks-style hotel in which the agency had been able to place them in Brooklyn. It would be up to him to work out the details with us.

The meeting went well. The parents were middle-aged, well groomed and polite, clearly upper middle-class. It soon became obvious that we were the ones being interviewed. The father explained that he was seeking a safe and kind home for Michi, aged sixteen, and Kimi, aged eighteen, during their adjustment period after three years in an internment camp. They would be learning American customs and he must be sure they would be the proper ones. They were not, he explained, servant class, but they had been taught basic household skills while in the internment camp. They were intelligent, anxious to learn and to please, he assured me.

Kimi and Michi proved to be all he said and more. They were Nisei, both having been born in the United States. The father had explained this during our interview, also that he was in reality both their uncle and stepfather, having married their mother, the widow of his brother. A few days later when the parents brought the girls to stay I felt sorry for everyone. They had themselves under such rigid control. How anxious the mother must have been for her children, how frightened the two young girls. I was apprehensive too. Could I reassure them, make them feel protected and at home? Would the experiment work? Sarah was, of course, delighted, Mother was interested and kind, and in a few days we were all friends.

Kimi became my assistant in the kitchen. I taught her some simple cooking and how to serve the family meals. She taught me how to brew tea properly and cook rice the never-failing Japanese way. Michi did the laundry. For six people, that was considerable. She also was a companion for Sarah, and when I was absent took charge of her and became her playmate. Together the two girls did the housecleaning. It was a much-needed breathing spell for me after the years of no help.

The reactions of our neighbors were interesting. Some applauded,

others thought it unpatriotic. Several of my friends with a houseful
of small children and no help were envious. One man, the father of a
friend of Sarah's, sent word that his daughters could only come over
when I was in the house and could watch. "Those Japs are not to be
trusted," I quote that particular Phi Beta Kappa as saying.

One very distressing incident occurred while the girls lived with
us. It was my custom to give Kimi and Michi their days off duty
together, though it was less convenient for me than having one of
them always available. I did not want either of them to be alone on
what might be hostile streets. On one of their afternoons off I had
retired after dinner, with a good book, to the comfort of the big four-
poster bed. I was suddenly interrupted by the sound of running feet
and the cries of two frightened children kneeling by my bed. They
kept saying, "We go to Mama." Slowly I got the story. They had
taken the bus to nearby White Plains for a picture show. When they
came out of the theater it was dark and they had been attacked by a
roaming bunch of hoodlums. Bombarded by cries of "dirty Japs"
and other obscenities, they had been chased down the street. Somehow they made it to the bus stop and home.

We all tried to reassure and comfort them. Even little Sarah understood enough to be angry. In spite of their cries for "Mama," I finally
made them understand they must go to bed and sleep. They could
decide in the morning. I went with them to their room and helped
them get ready for the night. The house quieted down and my husband and I were just ready to turn out the light when there was
another rush of feet, the door burst open, and I was hugged with
cries of "Mrs. Barber, we stay with you." For the remainder of the
months they lived with us I never quite lost the feeling that I had not
one but three daughters.

That experience had broken down barriers, and as they became
more sure of my affection I learned much about them. When their
father died his body had been cremated. It was decided that Michi
should take his ashes back to Japan, have a visit with her grandparents, and get to know her heritage and culture. She must have
been very young, maybe ten or twelve. I suppose a relative or friend

of the family accompanied her; she never said. When it became evident that World War II was spreading and we might be drawn into the conflict her parents sent for her and the two older brothers, who were also in Japan. She was allowed to leave, but the boys were approaching conscription age, and the government would not let them go. At the time Kimi and Michi were with us they had heard no word of them since the United States had entered the war, and had no way of knowing if they were still alive.

Kimi, the older sister, was pretty and very bright. We sometimes talked about the samenesses and differences of our two cultures. Once when I asked if she had enjoyed her free Sunday, she replied that she had gone to church. Remembering the Methodist connection, I asked if she had gone to a church in Brooklyn. No, she had gone to the Buddhist temple in upper west-side Manhattan. I said I didn't know anything about Buddhism; what was her religion like? "Like your Christianity, Mrs. Barber," Kimi said. I felt a gentle rebuke.

Kimi had a sweetheart in the European theater of operations from whom she heard infrequently. Like her, he was a Nisei and was a member of the 442nd Regimental Combat Team of the 100th Infantry Battalion. The men of that unit covered themselves with glory in the fighting in Italy. Since after Pearl Harbor their loyalty had been questioned, they were doubly anxious to prove it. They were ruthless attackers and their casualties were extremely high. They were known for their "go for broke" spirit. After months of a stalemate at the Abbey of Monte Cassino they broke the back of the German resistance which had blocked the Allied advance on Rome. Some fighting continued but for practical purposes the battle for Italy was finished. The 442nd Combat Team continued with the 5th Army into France and finally faced the Germans again in Germany. No Nisei was ever convicted of treason.

My brother Mat came home from Europe shortly after V-E Day in May, 1945. We asked him to spend his terminal leave with us before he returned to Florida and his prewar job. I wondered how the visit would go. I underestimated them all. Mat was by nature the most gentle of people. He was just glad to be alive and home. He didn't want to think of war, much less talk about it. The Japanese girls were glad he was safe and had not been wounded. Michi immediately appropriated his duffel bag of soiled clothes and disappeared into the laundry room. It was summer, and Mat was wearing his cotton uniforms. She saw to it that he had a freshly washed and ironed outfit every day of his visit. Kimi baked him an apple pie, her first. At dinner she put it before me with a flourish. It looked beautiful. Suddenly her face went blank. "Mrs. Barber, no sugar," she gasped. Everyone laughed. It set the tone for a happy, relaxed visit.

Several days after Mat arrived we were all sitting on the porch having a drink and waiting for dinner. The radio was playing soft music. Suddenly a voice broke in announcing the Japanese surrender. The war was over. Red turned to me and said, "You must go and tell them." I didn't know what to expect. Kimi was busy cooking, and Michi was helping. I said quietly, "Girls, the war is over, Japan has surrendered." I can still hear Kimi's gentle voice saying, "We are glad the killing is over."

Dinner was forgotten. Mother and Sarah, Mat and Red and I got in the car to make the hour's drive into New York to see the spectacular lights come on again in Times Square.

As soon as restrictions were lifted and the family could return to the West Coast, the parents came to reclaim their daughters. My idyll was over. How we all missed Kimi and Michi. At Christmas they sent me a lovely Japanese lacquer demitasse set, and about a year later we received an invitation to Kimi's wedding. It was written in Japanese on one side of the parchment and English on the other. I was glad to know that things worked out for her and her Nisei sweetheart.

Their time with us had been a learning experience for our family, particularly our very young Sarah. She has always been able to accept people for who they are inside, not because of an accidental pigmentation of skin. It was a great help during the nine years she taught second and third grades in Harlem. I am proud that she is truly color blind.

The departure of Kimi and Michi put me back on the "help wanted" treadmill. I can now recall one episode with a wry chuckle. During an interview I was trying to explain to a possible prospect that because of my husband's profession our routine had to be elastic. A dinner hour could be delayed by a doubleheader or an extra-inning game, a commuting train could be missed, and so on. She looked me in the eye and said, "I'se used to working for the quality, but I reckons I can work for the sporting folks too." She was wrong. After a few days' trial we parted company.

THE OPEN ROAD

The war was over at last. The harsh restrictions were finished. Travel was again possible. The mood of the country was a happy one. The ball clubs were free again to go south for spring training. In 1946 Mr. Rickey took the Dodgers to Daytona Beach. Sarah was only nine years old, and it was no great problem to take her out of school for several weeks.

Gasoline was again plentiful. We decided to make a real vacation of the trip south and left Scarsdale a week before training camp was to open. Red wanted to go by Lilesville, North Carolina, to see his aunt Virginia, who had nursed his father so lovingly in his last illness. We spent a couple of days in Columbus, Mississippi, where he had been born. We drove around the campus of Mississippi State College for Women, where Sarah's grandmother had been an entering student when she was sixteen years old. We visited a childhood friend of Red's mother who took Sarah up a winding stairway to a room on a wide landing where they had played as children. It was all very nostalgic. We wanted our New York daughter to feel that she was also, by heredity, a child of the South.

We continued on to New Orleans. Red had been there before; he had broadcast a Sugar Bowl New Year's game in 1940, but I had never seen the Crescent City. He said, "I want to take you to Antoine's for Oysters Rockefeller." I was willing. By accident we arrived for the start of Mardi Gras. The town was packed, but his CBS radio connections got us a room and tickets in a reviewing stand for the evening parade. Canal Street is a two-way avenue with a wide median strip. Platforms for viewing the parade had been erected along the way. It was barely dusk when we climbed up to our places. We waited and waited. A couple of hours went by. We were all getting tired and cross. Sarah sat down on the floor, leaned against her father's legs, and dozed. The other people were New Orleanians and assured us nothing like this had ever happened before. Finally the parade got under way. The floats, most elaborate, representing various social clubs of the city, came by. They were lighted from torches held by black men, boys really, clad in white loincloths who ran barefooted alongside the floats. We finally found out the cause of the delay. The torchbearers, at the last moment, had struck for higher wages. The negotiations were long and hectic, but the torchbearers finally won. The union movement had come to New Orleans. When we finally got to Antoine's it was still open. I got my first Oysters Rockefeller, but I think I would have had more zest for them a few hours earlier.

The following day we drove on to Tallahassee, where I had been such a happy college student. The next morning we drove out to the campus. I had intended, when we got there, to go into the Kappa Alpha Theta chapter house, and perhaps take Sarah in. We parked across the street, and I just sat there. Finally Red asked, "Aren't you going in?" "No," I said. I suddenly realized that the girls then in the house had been, at the time I lived there, just babies, two to five years old. It was too much of a difference in age. What did we have to say to each other?

Twenty-five years were to pass before I would see Tallahassee again. When we came back in 1972 to make the city our retirement home, the old sorority house was gone. The land on which it had stood is now a parking lot across the street from the entrance to the campus.

Our odyssey completed, we finally arrived in Daytona Beach for spring training. The living accommodations for the officials of the Dodgers, the owners, and the press and radio were in a rambling resort hotel, right on the ocean. Like most resort hotels in Florida at that time, except for the Gold Coast at Miami Beach (Fort Lauderdale was just beginning to grow), the clientele at the hotel was largely middle-aged or elderly.

Leo Durocher was manager of the Dodgers and at the height of his career. He was brash and noisy but capable and full of charm. He was also a skillful card player who loved the game of bridge. It was something to see him evenings, sitting at a bridge table with three

Left to right: Red, Pee Wee Reese, Leo Durocher, and Branch Rickey.

dowagers, charming them and probably taking their money. He was also stage-struck and was often surrounded by "show-biz" people.

Spring training in Mr. Rickey's years was very much family-oriented. It was a last chance for families with children still young enough to take out of school for a few weeks to be together before the long grind of the season. It was the time before the lonely road trips set in. Camp was well populated with families, and here Leo shone. He was genuinely fond of children and very easy with them.

Sarah had friends her own age. Mike and Hazel Gavin (he covered sports for the now defunct New York *Journal-American*) brought their Betty, who was the same age, and for a few years they were fast springtime friends. Jim and Dearie Mulvey (she had inherited her father's one-fourth interest in the Dodgers) came with their two daughters, both a little older than Sarah. Anne, the younger and very pretty, later married Ralph Branca. Baseball fans will remember him as the Dodger pitcher who threw that ill-fated home-run ball to Bobby Thomson of the Giants in the 1951 play-off game, which put the Giants in the World Series against the Yankees. Branca was never again to be as effective. As Casey Stengel said later, "That feller is still shell-shocked."

Walter O'Malley, a Brooklyn lawyer, had bought a one-fourth interest in the club. He and Kay, his wife, brought Peter, Sarah's age, and Terry, a daughter, who was a little older. As I remember that was a rainy spring, and Peter and Sarah spent much of their time playing the pinball machines in the hotel recreation room. Peter is now part owner and president of the Los Angeles Dodgers dynasty that his father, who died in 1980, built. Sarah is now an English professor at La Guardia College, part of the City University of New York.

When Ed Murrow came back from London after his distinguished years as a war correspondent, William S. Paley made him vice-president in charge of news for the entire CBS network. Sports at that time was in the news department. A few days after Murrow's arrival in New York, Ted Husing, one of the all-time great sports announcers, quit his job as director of sports at CBS to freelance. Murrow brought Red in to succeed Husing as director of sports. It soon became apparent that between the actual broadcasting of sporting events and his new role as administrative director of a department for the network, my husband could no longer afford the time required to commute into New York from Scarsdale. Finding an apartment for the family in the city became my assignment.

In July of 1946 such an assignment was not an easy one. New York was still under World War II rent control. There had been no new construction for the duration of the war. (The house we built in Scarsdale and moved into in January after Pearl Harbor had been the builder's last one.) My search seemed to be down one blind alley after another. The address, 1035 Fifth Avenue (Fifth Avenue and 85th Street), was really handed to us by Lady Luck. Margaret, the wife of Bill McCaffrey, who was Red's agent for many years, on her way home from work (she was secretary to John Royal, long-time vice-president of NBC, for whom Red had done several World Series broadcasts) had stopped in a cocktail lounge. She was joined by a

friend who, like Red, was a client of McCaffrey's, and in the course
of their visit he mentioned that an old lady who lived in his building
had died and her apartment was for rent. That evening Margaret
telephoned us about the apartment. Needless to say, we were at the
manager's office early the next morning.

The apartment was beautiful. It was on the fourteenth floor, di-
rectly across Fifth Avenue from the Metropolitan Museum, with a
view of Central Park stretching from the tall buildings on 59th Street
to the end of the park on 110th Street. We could see down the length
of 85th Street to the Hudson River. The city reservoir looked like a
lake from our windows. Not only was the apartment beautiful, it was
huge, larger actually than our house in the country which we were
leaving. Counting a servant's wing with three small bedrooms and a
sitting room, there were thirteen rooms and five baths. The space
was a luxury, but with a three-generation family, a live-in maid, and
always a cat or two it was wonderfully comfortable. Also, it was the
only apartment available. Because rent control was still in force there
was no negotiation on price: $400 a month!

In many ways the four-and-a-half years at 1035 Fifth were the
richest of my life. Certainly it was the most exciting period I've experienced. Everything was on the upswing. My husband's career was
expanding rapidly and in interesting ways. The city itself was a constant delight. There were the great shops on Fifth Avenue and the
multiple art galleries on Madison. The opera and the legitimate theaters in the Broadway area were only a quick bus ride from our front
door. The great Metropolitan Museum was directly across the street.
When our Sarah, who had no brothers, began expressing curiosity
about the physical differences between the sexes I took her for an
afternoon visit to the Museum and saw to it that we spent considerable time in the Greek wing with the life-size beautiful marble statues. A cop-out on my part, I suppose, but the best I could do with
my inherited reticence.

Then there was Mary Burke from County Mayo, who came to live
in that servants' wing as cook and general helper. She was in her

Red at CBS microphone.

early forties, I would guess, and had good Irish looks: black hair, vivid blue eyes, and high coloring. Mary had come to America as an immigrant when she was fourteen years old and gone to work in the only field open to an untrained girl, domestic service. She had spent years in the brownstone mansions of New York's upper East Side working for the wealthy members of New York society. She had been everything: scullery maid, laundress, housecleaner, children's nurse, ladies' maid, and even cook. (She was a versatile and superb cook.) By her own confession, she had grown too old and set in her ways to work in a situation with a number of fellow servants. We were the first household, she said, in which she would be the only live-in help.

Be that as it may, I soon found out that Mary had a friend who was an excellent laundress who "just happened" to have one free day. The building in which we lived did not have central air conditioning, and in the good weather when we opened windows, the city dust would come in, despite those fourteen stories. One day I complained that there was dust in the corners of the rooms. Mary replied in that rich County Mayo brogue which it had taken me several weeks to fully understand, "To the Irish all rooms are round." Soon after Mary settled in, another friend of hers, Nellie, began coming once a week to do heavy cleaning. In the large apartment she was actually needed, and I enjoyed the pleasant order that Mary brought about, even as I began to realize that I was being manipulated, in a quiet way, into what Mary considered proper under the circumstances for a lady in my situation.

On winter afternoons when I would come into the apartment after shopping, or perhaps after my "odd Fridays" at the symphony, Mary would appear in the library with a cup of hot tea and remark, "A lady should have a cup of tea in her own house." She did pamper me, and I purred. When my husband was out of town on professional assignments, as he often was, she would appear at my bedroom door with a breakfast tray. I do not care for breakfast in bed, but I tried to be gracious. I couldn't let Mary down.

She was indulgent, but she could also be severe. I remember the summer that Sarah and I spent several weeks in Westhampton.

Dorsey Ivey, a native of Savannah, Georgia, and mother of one of Sarah's classmates at Spence School, and I had taken rooms together in a sort of boardinghouse arrangement, a block or so away from the beach club. We had one another for company, and our little girls played and swam together in the ocean. There wasn't much to do during the weekdays except sun and swim at the beach, watch after the little girls, take long afternoon naps, read, and eat those great meals. The place we stayed in was noted for its excellent food.

When Sarah and I returned to the apartment Mary inquired about how the vacation had gone. "Fine," I said, "except I ate too much and I've gotten fat. You must help me lose these extra pounds." "Yes," she replied, "I've been meaning to speak to you. I've worked for several ladies who got fat and lost their husbands. Most of them weren't worth keeping anyway, but you have a good man. Don't let him go." If her remarks were a little fresh, they certainly kept me on a diet until the pounds were gone. I really didn't have much choice: The potatoes, desserts, and other goodies just never reached my end of the table.

Mary was always indulgent with Sarah. They formed an immediate alliance. That first morning when Mary appeared, suitcase in hand, to live with us I showed her to her quarters. I left her to settle in and, I hoped, to get to feel a little at home. How sad, I thought, to spend one's life getting used to being a stranger in another woman's home. I gave her an hour or so to adjust and then went back to see how things were going. No Mary! Well, I thought, great while it lasted. Still, when I looked in the dresser, it was obvious that she had unpacked. A few minutes later she was back, hands full of comic books for Sarah. I didn't have the heart to say I didn't approve of them. It wouldn't have done much good, I suspect. She spoiled Sarah outrageously, but I was grateful to Mary. My little girl had a hard enough adjustment to make coming from the casual freedom of life in Westchester County to the formal ritualized environment that was natural to the New York child who lived on the upper East Side and went to a private school.

After interviews at several schools I decided on Spence, one of the

Sarah with Mr. Walkie-Talkie, the Siamese cat.

older prestige girls' schools. It seemed a happy compromise between
Brearley, excellent academically but a bit blue-stocking, and Miss
Hewitt's, very social. I can never forget Sarah's first day at Spence.
School opened a week before we could move into the apartment, and
she and I stayed at the small residential hotel within easy walking
distance of school. After a hurried breakfast in the coffee shop at the
hotel, we set out for the walk to school. Sarah had eaten almost no

breakfast. I knew that meant she was uneasy, probably frightened. I wasn't in much better shape. When we arrived there was a long line of students waiting to greet Mrs. Osborne, the headmistress. As each little girl reached Mrs. Osborne she made a deep, proper dancing school curtsy. Poor Sarah had never seen, much less made, a curtsy. I said a silent fervent prayer: "Dear Lord, don't let her fall flat on her face." She didn't. Her effort was awkward but adequate. We had both survived our initiation into city life.

Our next crisis presented itself a few weeks later. One afternoon during the walk back to the apartment Sarah said to me, "Mother, all the other girls go to dancing class on Fridays. I want to go where Whitney goes." Whitney was the first friend Sarah had made at Spence. I had met Whitney's mother, and I telephoned for the particulars. "The Benjamin Classes," she said, "but I doubt there is a vacancy. You have to practically be born into them."

Red and I had become parishioners of St. James' Church at 71st Street and Madison Avenue, where Dr. Horace W. B. Donegan, who was later to become Bishop of the Diocese of New York, was rector. Harry Price, who was rector of Saint James' in Scarsdale where Red had been a vestryman for several years, was a personal friend of Dr. Donegan, and he had brought him to the apartment when we moved into town. We had become friendly acquaintances. Sarah's father enlisted his help. I don't know which "born into" parishioner he put the bite on, but Sarah received her invitation and the sports broadcaster's daughter became a member of the Benjamin Dancing Classes.

I took Sarah to her first dancing class, properly attired thanks to Whitney's mother's coaching. She looked small and pretty but so vulnerable in her party dress, short white sox, and black patent-leather Mary Jane shoes. The children came from schools all over the city. Would they be kind to the stranger? The dancers came in the care of mothers or governesses.

Most of the time I did errands during the class periods but sometimes I stayed and watched the antics from the wings. The girls in their party dresses and dancing slippers sat on the little gilt chairs waiting anxiously for some boy to come from the center of the floor and claim them as partners. Often there were a few more girls than boys and even then it was apparent who were going to be the girls left sitting on the gilt chairs. I felt sorry for them. The cards are stacked so soon. The boys, freshly scrubbed, looked like choirboys, but they were waiting to break loose. I was there the afternoon Andy, Sarah's best friend, brought a bag of red-painted pistachio nuts which he gleefully scattered over the dance floor to the dismay of the dancing master and the delight of the students.

I watched with an interested but amused eye. It all seemed so staged, but those little savages did learn good manners and acquired a certain ease, useful in strange social situations.

In 1948 CBS sent Red to Switzerland to broadcast the Winter Olympic Games in San Moritz. Red returned home by way of London where he stopped for a conference with the British Broadcasting Company. The flight from London stopped at Shannon, Ireland, and at Gander. We were still living in the apartment on Fifth Avenue and Mary Burke was with us. Knowing how homesick she sometimes got, Red decided that he would bring her a bag of dirt from Ireland. Mary grew plants in her room, and Red thought she would like to sprinkle a part of Ireland on them. He got the bag of dirt at the airport, and things went well until he hit Customs at the Overseas Terminal at La Guardia. The inspector, who happened by luck to be Irish, asked, "What have you got there?" When Red explained it was soil from Shannon, the inspector said, "You can't take that in, the Department of Agriculture won't let you." Red explained, in detail, that he just wanted to take a "bit of the old sod" to Mary Burke, who was sometimes very homesick for the Emerald Isle. The immigrations officer finally threw up his hands and said, "Oh, the poor colleen, take the bag and get out of here." Red has said he considers that one of his best "broadcasts," maybe his best. When we closed the apartment in New York, Mary took the pot of Irish soil with her.

There are so many highlights from those years at 1035 Fifth, but one episode has to be outstanding. Ethel Barrymore came to New York the fall of 1949 to be an honored guest of ANTA (the American National Theater Academy) and to have a part in one of their benefit efforts. During her stay she celebrated her seventieth birthday and Leonard Lyons gave her a birthday party. He was at that time a columnist for the *New York Post* and did a theater column called "The Lyons Den." Miss Barrymore was an avid baseball fan, and when Lyons asked her whom she would like for guests she named two people: Joe DiMaggio and Red Barber.

When we arrived at the Lyons' apartment on Central Park West, Miss Barrymore was already there. No other guests had yet arrived and for a while I sat beside her on a small sofa. She had on a severe black dress, sort of schoolmarmish. I thought immediately of having seen her on Broadway for opening night of *The Corn Is Green*, her successful play about a Welsh schoolteacher. She was gracious, apologizing for being a little under the weather with a head cold. To me she was perfect. The hands were those of an older woman, but the expressive face and the beautiful deep voice were young. Her hair was completely gray, but the famous Barrymore profile was still firm in the alive white face.

All evening the greats from the world of the theater kept coming and going. Some had to leave early because they were in current shows, some could only come late, after the evening performances were finished, but most, like the Barbers, came at the invited hour and stayed. All were there to do honor to the great lady of their profession. I was excited and dazzled by the occasion, which seemed almost unreal to me.

We sat in groups of four at card tables. Miss Barrymore had her two specially requested guests, Red and DiMaggio, on either side. Herbert Bayard Swope, a famous newspaper reporter and editor, made a fourth. He had been a beau of the guest of honor during her early years in the theater. I didn't do so badly myself. I sat at the table with playwright William Saroyan and John Steinbeck, the author of *The Grapes of Wrath*. He brought with him a pretty young redhead, who later became his wife. The two writers exchanged ideas and episodes. The young redhead and I made an attentive and fascinated audience.

All during the evening the late guests kept arriving. Leonard Bernstein came with his sister. He and Frank Loesser entertained us at the piano with their four hands. They gave impromptu snatches of their then-unpublished melodies. I think I heard themes that were later to become famous in *West Side Story*, but memory may be tricking me. Abe Burroughs accompanied himself on the piano in original comedy skits. Eddie Albert came in after the show in which he was then performing. Ezio Pinza, starring in *South Pacific*, came late. He was obviously tired after his demanding evening performance and did not stay long. A buffet table was set up for the latecomers. When Red and I left long after midnight the room was still crowded. They kept coming, the well known of the entertainment world, to pay homage to Ethel Barrymore.

An opening night on Broadway has a magic all its own. During our years of living in New York we only attended three, but what a threesome they were. Ethel Barrymore in *The Corn Is Green* (as best I can remember this was her last appearance on Broadway); Pinza, reigning bass-baritone of the Metropolitan Opera, opening with Mary Martin in *South Pacific*; and Art Carney in *The Rope Dancers*. Barrymore opened in a snowstorm, but the house was packed, a tribute to the great lady. Tickets to opening nights are at a premium, and when I said to Red that I wanted to go to the opening of *South Pacific*, he gave a gasp and said, "I'll try." He appealed to Bill McCaffrey, his agent, who also represented Mary Martin. Bill tried—no luck. Red then asked Robert Russell Bennett, who orchestrated the music for the show and was in Boston with the cast for the tryouts. Red had narrated the fourth movement of Bennett's "Symphony in D for the Dodgers" which the New York Philharmonic Orchestra had performed in Lewisohn Stadium several seasons before. He also had, upon occasion, left complimentary tickets for Bennett and his grandson for games at Ebbets Field. Bennett, with chagrin, said, "I can't get any." In desperation and as a last resort,

Red appealed to Zak Becker, who was financial, pension, and labor negotiator for CBS where Red was then sports director. CBS had bought a piece of *South Pacific*. Zak said, "It's late. I'll try, but they won't be good." "Just so they are in the theater," Red replied. So they were, the next to last row downstairs, but they were center, and for a musical that's not bad. When we reached the theater that night there was a big black Cadillac limousine parked at the curbing square in front of the door. It belonged to William S. Paley, president of CBS. At intermission he and Mrs. Paley and their guests sat in the car and had drinks. The Barbers were not invited.

I was fortunate; I saw *South Pacific* four times, and the two principals were performing every time. Pinza missed a number of shows but not one of mine. I took Sarah to a matinee. She is quite musical, and at that time was singing in schoolgirl performances at Spence School. Bill McCaffrey had told Mary Martin that Sarah and I would be at the afternoon show. She was gracious and invited us to come backstage to her dressing room after the show. She asked Sarah what she wanted to do when she grew up. "Be an actress like you, but I get a stomach ache when I have to sing solo." "I do too," Mary replied. She went on to say, "That's because we are artists. I got a stomach ache before the curtain went up this afternoon, but, see, I'm all right now." How kind she was, a busy, successful actress, to take the time to reassure a child. The words stood Sarah in good stead a few weeks later when at Spence School she sang the soprano role in *Pirates of Penzance*. Three days before the scheduled performance Sarah fell and broke her arm, but, cast and all, she sang, and sang well.

My third opening night, Art Carney in *The Rope Dancers*, was actually the most interesting. Carney was also a client of Bill McCaffrey's, and we knew Art and his wife Jean. Bill and Margaret had invited us to join them and the Carneys at Sardi's after the performance to wait for the early editions of the papers with their reviews of the opening. In those years Sardi's Restaurant was the great hangout for people of the theater. Sidney Fields, who wrote the column "Only Human" for the *New York Daily News*, and his wife Dorothy joined us. Dorothy, at the time, was secretary for McCaffrey. Later in the evening Sidney phoned his paper and the *New York Times* and came back with the news that, on the whole, the reviews were favorable. To celebrate, we all drank a toast, "To Art and a long run," and went home to bed. Opening night was over.

There were so many exciting firsts for me in those New York years. I am not a boxing fan. My only exposure to the sport (if it can be called that) had been when Red was working at WRUF, the University of Florida radio station, and doing the college amateur bouts and an occasional professional fight in the small town of Gainesville. Both events were free to me, and that kind of entertainment was a big plus in those days. Still, the inducement of the "big show" is different. Bill McCaffrey seemed always to have contacts in the varied facets of the show world, and when he invited me to go with him and Margaret to the Joe Louis–Tami Mauriello fight September 18, 1946 at Yankee Stadium, I was delighted. Red had an evening show and could not go with us. The stadium was packed and getting down to our front seats was slow going. The fight began just as we reached our seats but we were still standing in the aisle when Joe let go with a lethal punch and bang—a first-round knockout. Since then I have taken my prize fights before the television screen.

MR. RICKEY MEANT BUSINESS

Spring training and a new season are always a time of excitement for baseball people. There are friends to be seen again after the separation of the winter months. There is a sense of anticipation. What will this year be like? Will it be a good spring training with warm sunny weather? Will the club have a successful year?

Of the many years that I was part of the baseball world there are three spring trainings that I remember most vividly. They all have to do with Mr. Rickey's decision to challenge the color ban and bring Jackie Robinson to play ball for Brooklyn.

Mr. Rickey stood alone when he signed Robinson. He placed Jackie on the Montreal roster for 1946. Montreal then was the top farm club in the Brooklyn organization, and Mr. Rickey reasoned correctly that Jackie would be better received in Montreal for his first season than anywhere in the United States. There were too many problems then in the South, too many laws against integration, too much prejudice.

Mr. Rickey knew when to make a move, and he knew also when to wait before making the next move. For spring training of 1947 he took both the Montreal and Brooklyn clubs to Havana, Cuba. I remember this spring training. The Dodgers stayed at the elegant Hotel National. Our rooms overlooked the Malecón and the harbor. The weather was beautiful, one sunny day after another, and the old city was fun to explore. Red rented a car, and he and Sarah and I enjoyed several trips into the countryside.

Ernest Hemingway was living in Cuba at the time with Mary Welsh, the war correspondent, his fourth and last wife. He often came to the exhibition games. He was fascinated by the ball players, another sign of his macho associations, and from time to time would invite them to his finca.

I remember one evening in 1947 when, after a night game, Red and I dropped in at the Floridida Bar for a nightcap. Ernest and

Mary came in and joined us at our table. He and Red had become
acquainted at the training sessions at the ball park. Mary did not
know either of us and at first was guarded, but she relaxed when she
realized we had no ax to grind. I remember that Hemingway sipped
Cointreau which he followed with sips of ice-cold soda water. The
talk was great and went on well into the small hours. His two sons,
who seemed quite accustomed to such a routine, slept in his station
wagon parked outside the bar.

Hemingway always wanted to be regarded as a strong, virile,
rough, two-fisted male animal. I wasn't with the Dodgers when they
trained in Havana in 1942, when MacPhail had the ball club. World
War II was on and only the ball players, the club officials, and the
working press made the trip to Cuba. When Red got home he told
me of an episode that was most revealing about Hemingway's macho
complex.

Hemingway hung around the ball players at the hotel, took them
to shoot pigeons, and finally invited a group of the Dodgers to his
finca for an evening's entertainment. The first thing Hemingway did
was to bring out a set of boxing gloves, and he insisted that the big
relief pitcher, Hugh Casey, put them on and spar with him. This is
what Casey told Red the next morning.

"I didn't want to put on the gloves . . . I'd done some professional
fighting years ago. But he wouldn't let me alone. He kept demanding I put on the gloves . . . that we'd just spar a little bit. Finally I
put them on, and instead of sparring he began hitting me. I told him
to stop hitting me, and with that he really hit me. So I knocked
him down."

When Casey floored Hemingway it made quite a racket. The then-
Mrs. Hemingway, Martha Gellhorn, stormed down from upstairs
and ordered everybody out of the house. Pronto. The party was over.

The end of the Hemingway story came, for me, years later. In
1967 after thirty-three consecutive years of broadcasting major
league baseball, my husband was for the first time able to take a long
summer vacation. We started from Key Biscayne in a brand-new
Lincoln Continental (only 400 miles on the speedometer) to fulfill

Red's dream that the first time he was free from baseball, he would buy a new car and drive to the Rocky Mountains, with no time schedule. On our leisurely rambling we found ourselves in Sun Valley, Idaho. We stayed a night at the big resort hotel. It was off-season and the hotel was almost empty. We stopped in the bar for a predinner drink. Except for the bartender, we were the only people there. My husband, who is by nature and training an enquiring reporter, engaged him in conversation. The bartender talked long about Hemingway, how he had spent much time in the bar, and pointed out to us the secluded table at which he had done some of his writing. He told us how Hemingway's death had shocked the community and that he was buried in the town cemetery in nearby Ketchum. The next morning Red and I drove over. The cemetery was well kept but quite bare. It was on a hill. There were no big trees. The grave lay at the crest of the hill—a plain, dark granite slab. The simple inscription read:

Ernest Hemingway
1899–1961

What it did not say was "dead by his own hand."

Back to 1947 and spring training in Havana. It was during that stay that MacPhail and Rickey came to their final explosive parting of the ways. The trouble came in part from Leo Durocher's fascination with show people. Commissioner Happy Chandler, the ex-governor of Kentucky and ex-United States senator who succeeded Judge Landis as commissioner of baseball, had warned Leo about his close association with George Raft, the actor, and Raft's gambler friends. Branch Rickey, for his part, was exercised over having seen two well-known gamblers in what he believed was Larry MacPhail's box at a Dodger-Yankee exhibition game. He exploded to the writers, asking, "Are there two sets of rules in the commissioner's office, one for Leo and the Dodgers and another for MacPhail and the Yankees?" MacPhail's response was immediate, and equally heated. He denied that the gamblers were in his box or that he even knew them, much less having them there as his guests, and stated that he had no control over who bought tickets to baseball games. The fat was in the fire.

Rickey and MacPhail had already been feuding because of Mac-Phail's hiring of Dodger coaches Charlie Dressen and Red Corriden. The Dodgers and Dressen had reached a verbal agreement for the forthcoming season, and Rickey charged MacPhail with having induced Dressen to violate it. It was also reported that Larry had sought to hire away Durocher to manage the Yankees.

Leo had for some weeks been in the public eye because of his marriage to the actress Laraine Day. Laraine had received a divorce from her husband in California, with instructions from the judge that she was not to remarry in that state for one year. Shortly afterward she and Leo had gone to Mexico and been married. The judge in California reacted with public accusations of adultery, and Leo had responded in kind. The affair drew much publicity, and one Catholic youth group in Brooklyn announced that henceforth its young members would not be permitted to attend Dodger games.

Shortly after Rickey had made his remarks about the gamblers who were supposedly MacPhail's guests, Leo—in a byline newspaper column ghostwritten by Harold Parrott, which he probably hadn't even read—sounded off on the MacPhail incident. The uproar resulted in Chandler holding two hearings over the charges and countercharges, and then announcing that MacPhail and Dressen were being fined, and that Durocher, for conduct detrimental to baseball, was suspended for one year.

As a result the Dodgers opened the 1947 season without a manager. Coach Clyde Sukeforth managed the first two games, and then Mr. Rickey brought his old friend Burt Shotten out of retirement in Bartow, Florida, to finish the season. The club won the pennant. To make the irony complete, they lost in the World Series to MacPhail's Yankees.

I have another vivid memory of that spring in Havana. One day Red, Sarah, and I—anxious to learn as much as we could about Cuba while we had the opportunity—drove into the non-tourist interior of the island. We went through several small villages straddled along the highway near the big sugar fields owned, for the most part, by United States sugar corporations. The villages were home for the peasants who worked the fields. The primitive conditions and the poverty were beyond belief. I cannot forget the naked children with their swollen bellies, the result of malnutrition, maybe even starvation, standing along the road watching us pass. They did not seem even to have the energy for play. Later I understood well why Castro's revolution overthrew Batista's dictatorship. In a country where everyone was either very rich or very poor, what did the poor have to lose?

It was in late March of 1945 when I learned Mr. Rickey had made up his mind to end the color line in baseball. I knew that Red had a luncheon date with Mr. Rickey at Joe's Restaurant in Brooklyn, but I certainly was not prepared for the bombshell my husband brought home with him. Nor was I prepared for his reaction.

He blurted, "Mr. Rickey just told me he is going to bring a Negro player to the Brooklyn Dodgers. He swore me to strict secrecy but said I could tell you. I don't think I can go through with that. I think I'll have to quit!"

I was surprised by the intensity of his reaction, but in a way I understood. Born in Mississippi, raised in redneck Central Florida, and educated at the all-male, all-white University of Florida he had been, as the song in *South Pacific* went, "carefully taught."

All I could think to say was, "Well, you don't have to quit tonight . . . let's have a martini." By next morning his innate sense of fair play, kindness, and intelligence had taken over. He began to ask himself, "What choice did I have in the color I was born?" Also he began to realize that it was a mighty fine job he was contemplating walking away from.

My reaction was low-key and different. By circumstance I too had been "carefully taught." My mother, after my father's death, when I was five and my brother was three, by necessity had gone to work as a secretary. The daily care of her two young children was dependent upon a black nurse who sometimes brought her own child, of a comparable age, as a playmate. It seemed quite natural to me. When I became a student nurse at Riverside Hospital, Eugene Matthews was chief orderly, and was black. He was so kind and helpful to us frightened, timid probationers. After my mother's remarriage it was Henry, the black combination chauffeur, yardman, and heavy cleaner, who often softened my stepfather's harshness. Once when my stepfather was on a prolonged business trip Henry taught Mother to drive the car. His kindnesses, if discovered, would certainly have cost him his job.

When Mr. Rickey made his decision known to Red it offered no emotional challenge to me. I admired his courage and hoped it would not be too difficult for him. And I knew Red would get his thinking straightened out—which he quickly did.

When 1947 came and Robinson joined the Dodgers, he encountered much hostility. My husband's swift adjustment to the rightness of Mr. Rickey's brave move was not matched by all baseball people, or for that matter by the American public in general. There were many whites to whom the breaking down of the color line in the national sport was a harsh and bitter pill to swallow.

One couple, longtime friends from our early married days in Gainesville, Florida, called and said they were in New York for several days. We invited them to come to the apartment for dinner. The visit went very well. Later in the evening Red suggested they might like to be his guests for some Dodgers games at Ebbets Field. Our friend, a practicing lawyer, and from one of the old families in Gainesville, exploded.

"No. I'll never set foot in Ebbets Field as long as that nigger is playing there!"

Red didn't hesitate. He softly replied, "We won't miss you."

The evening was over. We never saw them again.

In 1948 Mr. Rickey took the Dodgers to the Dominican Republic for spring training. By then Jackie Robinson was an established member, a star of the team, but he could not train with the club in then-segregated Florida. I was so excited. Would I be able to go, to see for myself the island of Hispaniola, so rich in history, and stand on the very spot where Columbus first set foot in the New World? Red, of course, would go. It was his business, but could I take Sarah out of school for a month and the two of us go with him? By then we were living in New York City, and Sarah was a student at Spence School. Mrs. Osborne, the headmistress, was understanding; she felt it would be a fine opportunity for Sarah, provided I took her school books and tutored her for an hour or so in the mornings.

We took a night flight to Puerto Rico, and after a short wait in the airport transferred to a smaller plane for the morning trip to Ciudad Trujillo. The name of the old capital city of Santo Domingo had been changed when Rafael Trujillo Molina became dictator of the country. The flight over the blue tropical water was beautiful, and we landed in bright sunlight. The Dodgers stayed at the Jaragua Hotel, at that time the only resort-type hotel in the city. Our suite opened onto a balcony that overlooked the pool and the hotel gardens and beyond the blue, blue Caribbean Sea. As soon as we checked in and were settled in our rooms a waiter appeared with a tray of delicious chilled tropical fruits and hot coffee. It had been sent by Tony Vaughan, manager of the hotel. We soon found out that the gesture was typical of his thoughtful hospitality.

Tony arranged many pleasant excursions for the Dodger family. There were short tours around the city in horse-driven carriages, quite a treat for Sarah, who had never seen one before except at home in Central Park. We went to the cathedral, the oldest in the Western world. Begun in 1514, the cathedral housed what was reputed to be the tomb of Christopher Columbus. On my first trip to Spain some years later, I was shown another tomb in which Columbus had presumably been interred and was assured that it was the authentic resting place of the great explorer. So much for historical authenticity; I shall assume between the two that I paid my respects to the right one.

The city itself, the oldest continuously inhabited in the Western world, had been established in 1496 by Bartholomew Columbus,

brother of Christopher. The old part of the city was small. It hugged
the banks of the Ozama River up which Columbus had sailed in
1492. Tourist guides were glad to point out to the visitor the exact
spot on which the explorer first set foot. More authenticity. In 1948
the streets were few and for the most part cobblestoned. The public
buildings shone white against the blue sea and sky. All the wooden
trim on them, and there was lots of it, including balconies, was
elaborately carved of the plentiful, indigenous Dominican ma-
hogany. History spoke out on every side. It was a wonderful opportunity for our daughter, who was just beginning to study about the
discovery and colonization of the New World.

We went to the cathedral for Palm Sunday Mass. The ritual was
impressive and the music magnificent, but we were disappointed that
the archbishop was not present. We had been told that he was very
old and not too well but we wanted to see him. He had been coura-
geous and outspoken in his disapproval of Trujillo's repressive regime, a daring thing to do in a dictatorship. When we returned to the
hotel Tony was in the lobby and asked how our visit was going. We
told him we had been to the cathedral but were disappointed to miss
the archbishop. Tony, who was a devout Roman Catholic, replied,
"He's a friend of mine, I'll take care of that."

He did. Two days later the invitation came for luncheon with Tony
and the archbishop in Tony's apartment; we were told to "be sure
and bring Sarah." When we arrived the other invited guests from the
hotel were there. They were Mr. and Mrs. Robert Moses and Mr.
and Mrs. Lou Crandall. Moses, at that time, was the powerful New
York City Parks Commissioner and Crandall was president of Fuller
Construction Corporation, which was then engaged in building a
large resort hotel in nearby Puerto Rico. We had a cocktail and
shortly thereafter Archbishop Riccardo Pittini arrived. He was fee-
ble, but in his episcopal robes he was most impressive. He was also
modest and charming. The archbishop was accompanied by a black
man who was a combination chauffeur, valet, and personal attendant.
By then the archbishop was almost completely blind, and I remember well the servant-friend's kind attention. He guided the old

man's shaky fork to his mouth and saw, so gently, that there were no mishaps.

After luncheon we visited with the honored guest for a while. He took Sarah on his lap. (An ecclesiastical robe does give a man a nice lap. I wonder if that is the reason an American priest I met once in Rome hated so to have to wear his cassock on the streets and in public places?) The archbishop said to our daughter, "You must always be a very good girl because you are the sun and moon in the firmament of your parents' happiness." I am sure she did not quite understand, but she was impressed and answered, "I will try."

During the luncheon the Crandalls and the Barbers found out, to our mutual surprise and pleasure, that we lived in the same apartment building in New York. Marguerite and Lou became our dear friends.

Another Dominican episode involved Mr. and Mrs. Rickey and "a day in the country." Mr. Rickey decided to take a day off from baseball, and he made plans to rent a car and driver and make the trip across the island to Santiago. There we'd have lunch and just explore. When the car arrived it was big and very comfortable for the five of us. The driver was, like the archbishop's attendant, dark black, noticeable in a country which was predominantly mulatto. Like the other black man, he spoke an almost Elizabethan English which was obviously his native tongue. Later, we learned their story. They came from a settlement of ex-slaves who had been brought by the Quakers from Philadelphia, which had been settled as a Quaker colony in 1681. They had been set free, but they chose to stay in their rather remote area and remained true to their Quaker training and carefully taught English tongue. They did not intermarry with the native Spanish-speaking mulattoes.

Our excursion started off in high gear. The weather was perfect, the frangipani trees were in full bloom, the countryside just mountainous enough to be interesting. When Mrs. Rickey inquired about the possibility of a restroom stop, the driver said he would stop at the house of "Trujillo's brother's keep lady on the way to Santiago." His Quaker voice held just the slightest tinge of disapproval of Trujillo's brother's travel arrangements. The lady's house sat at a curve in the road on the brow of a hill with a fine view. The house was new and the lady most obliging. I felt that this was not her first experience with such an emergency.

The next emergency our driver could not dispose of so easily. In late morning the car just stopped. Nothing he could do got it going. Finally, in desperation and some embarrassment, he hailed a passing cattle truck which happened, fortunately, to be empty of its usual occupants. He asked the driver to take us to the nearest village some five miles up the road and leave us at the restaurant on the square, where we could get lunch. He promised to come and get us as soon as he could get the car going. All thought of going to Santiago for lunch had vanished. All we wanted was to get somehow back to Ciudad Trujillo and civilization. Mrs. Rickey got in the front seat with the driver. The rest of us rode standing in the back. The going was rough and the truck had not been too thoroughly cleaned after its more traditional tenants, but we were glad at least to be on the move. Finally we reached the tiny village and the restaurant. When we went inside, the restaurant was empty and not too clean. The waiter who came was Chinese and spoke in the familiar sing-song English of New York's Chinatown. How do you suppose he got to the remote interior of that Caribbean island? The menu of the day he recited to us. It was some sort of Chinese dish, but the food was hot and thoroughly cooked and there was bottled Coca-Cola. We made do, but were relieved when our driver walked in.

We got in the car and headed back toward Ciudad Trujillo, but the misadventures of the day were not over. About an hour later the car stopped again. By this time we all were getting pretty frantic. We must have been a pathetic sight standing there on the side of the road. (If this begins to read like a bad script for a B-grade movie bear with me.) Our trip had become a nightmare to the five of us. But finally along came the happy ending, in the person of a Coca-Cola executive returning from a business trip to Santiago. He stopped, asked what was the trouble, and offered us a lift back to the hotel. He was well dressed and spoke cultured, unaccented English. We assumed him to be an American businessman stationed in the Republic. Red, always the reporter, asked, "You speak English, where do you come from?" The reply was, "I am a Dominican, but I was educated at an academy in Peekskill, New York." He told us he was married and that he and his wife had two little girls about Sarah's age. When he let us out at the hotel he gave Red and Mr. Rickey his business card, which included his home address and telephone number.

A few days later Red called and asked him if he and his wife would come with their daughters to the hotel for a visit. We wanted a chance to express our appreciation for his kindness. The family was most attractive, obviously upper class. The little girls and Sarah took to each other. Their mother brought her little blonde daughters several afternoons to swim with Sarah in the hotel pool. It was welcome company for Sarah, and the mother and I got to know each other as we sat in the garden and watched the children play. She told me much about what life was like for their class on the island, that it was a male-oriented society, and that there were many restrictions placed on her because she was a woman. She told me that it was not uncommon for a man to have two families, one with his wife, another with his mistress. It was a situation the wife was expected to accept, even to having the children of both women for the husband's birthday party. She said several of her friends had faced the problem, but she was fortunate, her husband was faithful—more like an American than a Latin husband.

Another planned luncheon party worked more smoothly but was every bit as interesting. Red and I decided that we should take advantage of proximity and see a little of the nearby French-speaking Black Republic (so called) of Haiti. We took the short midmorning flight from Ciudad Trujillo to Port-au-Prince, the capital city of Haiti. The difference was immediate and marked. Port-au-Prince was a shock. I have not been in India, where conditions are said to be even worse, but the poverty was appalling. Most of the people were barefooted, and their clothing was ragged and dirty. The town was no better. The shops offered little to entice a tourist. We had been

told, by Tony Vaughan I think it was, to take a taxi up into the hills
to Pétionville and have lunch at a little French restaurant where he
had eaten. On the way we passed the presidential palace. It was most
impressive, enormous, very white. It had lots of flags and was, I'm
sure, well guarded.

I know that the emigration of great numbers of Haitians to Miami
and South Florida in 1980 created a serious problem for that part of
the state. However, remembering what we saw in 1948 and having
seen later how little has changed for the peasants, I understand why
they risked their lives in those small, unseaworthy boats. They had
nothing to lose but their lives; and their existence has been so un-
bearably hard, the gamble was worth it.

In 1949, two years after Jackie Robinson had broken the color line
in baseball, Mr. Rickey took the Dodgers to Vero Beach for spring
training. He had secured the closed-down Naval Air Training Station on the outskirts of town. Our quarters were certainly not as
elaborate as they had been in the Dominican Republic. Most of the
players and the press and some of the office staff lived in the barracks
that had housed naval personnel during World War II. There were a
few small motel-type apartments, probably originally officers' quarters. They were occupied by some of the Dodger personnel who, like
my husband, had brought their families with them. The three of us
had two rooms and a bath but no kitchen facilities beyond a small
refrigerator. All our meals were taken in the common dining room in
the main building. There was a sort of recreation room equipped
with the usual pinball machines. On the grounds was a big swimming pool where the children spent a large part of their time.

Since the base was federal property and therefore not subject to
the laws of Florida, Mr. Rickey was free, for the first time, to take
Jackie Robinson to Florida to train with the rest of the Dodgers.
Jackie brought Mrs. Robinson and Jackie, Jr., who must have been
about three years old, with him. Mrs. Robinson was young, slender,
pretty, well groomed, and a lady. She had been a student at UCLA
with Jackie.

I have thought so often and wondered what that first spring in Florida, in a white, segregated society, must have been like for Mrs. Robinson. Years later, in his book *The Boys of Summer*, Roger Kahn told of asking her, "How did you find spring training in the South?" Her reply was, "Humiliating." I saw one example of it. The team played an exhibition game in West Palm Beach. A number of the players' wives went down, among them Mrs. Robinson. I went with Red. The ball park was in a rundown section of town, in miserable condition, a typical minor, minor league establishment. When Mrs. Robinson reached the entrance gate she was told by the ticket taker to go to the "colored gate." Later I heard what happened when she asked an usher where she could take her little boy to a restroom. The reply was abusive, obscene. I felt ashamed. I was indignant for her. How did she stand it?

On the base she was shielded. I hope she felt things were different for her. Certainly they were for little Jackie. In his childhood world there was no black or white. Mr. and Mrs. Rickey had brought their granddaughter with them. She was the same age as little Jackie, and they became constant companions. I remember the little boy so well. He looked very much like his mother and was always so well groomed, often dressed in a white sailor suit. With his big soft brown eyes he was a most appealing child.

Jackie Junior's life was to be tragic. It is not easy for an adolescent to be the child of a famous person. I know how our Sarah, in those years, suffered from and resented being "Red Barber's daughter." She wanted to be "Sarah Barber," her own person. Poor young Jackie, overshadowed by his father, the great athlete, the successful challenger of tradition and prejudice: How was he going to be as great? He went to war. He came back from Vietnam a heroin addict, as did so many young men. After a long struggle with drugs and treatment at Daytop in Seymour, Connecticut, things seemed to be getting straightened out. He was off drugs and trying to help other young people who had become addicts. He was killed at 2:30 A.M. on the Merritt Parkway in a one-car accident. We still refuse to learn—there are no good wars.

Spring training, 1949, was a short one for me. I could only take Sarah for the duration of her school's spring break, about ten days in all. The next year Sarah remained at home with Mary Burke in the apartment on Fifth Avenue, and Red and I stayed at a motel in Vero Beach. The base was changing, expanding, Rickey was laying the foundation on which O'Malley later built Dodgertown, the show-place of training camps, where the Los Angeles Dodgers train today. MacPhail and Rickey were innovators—shakers of the status quo. O'Malley was a developer, an expander.

Branch Rickey's last year as president of the Dodgers was 1950, but in the spring we didn't know that. O'Malley succeeded him as president at the end of the playing season. A brand-new baseball stadium had been built in Miami. The Dodgers opened it with a few exhibition games in 1950. Under O'Malley the club began playing many of its spring games in Miami. For the next three years, our last with the Dodgers, Red and I stayed at a villa at the then-new Key Biscayne Hotel. The island was just beginning to grow after the Rickenbacker Causeway had been completed, making it available for development. There were the hotel and villas, a single combination all-purpose store and post office, and a few scattered modest vacation cottages. The rest was coconut trees, beautiful beaches, the ocean, and sunshine. What a break it was, after the hard winters of New York State. It was not strange after those three pleasant springs that when in 1966 we decided to move for good out of the New York area, we would find a house on Key Biscayne.

MOTHERS AND DAUGHTERS

I was thirty-six years old when Mr. Rickey came to Brooklyn, and he was sixty-one, almost old enough to be my father. He and Mrs. Rickey had taken an apartment in Bronxville near where we were living in the house we had built in Scarsdale. Their first overture was to invite us for luncheon at a nearby restaurant. By the time the meal was over, we were friends. I often joined Mrs. Rickey and her sister, Miss Moulton, in Mrs. Rickey's box. Sarah was always welcome. Often Mary, Branch Jr.'s wife, was also there. It was like being a member of a family—something I had missed while growing up.

In 1945 Branch Rickey, Walter O'Malley, and John L. Smith each bought twenty-five percent ownership of the Dodgers. Jim Mulvey's wife Dearie had the remaining interest in the organization. Smith died shortly after the partnership was formed. O'Malley, as Mrs. Smith's lawyer, now had control of fifty percent of the ball club. He began putting the squeeze on Rickey, whose contract expired in 1950. In the final months of the 1950 season, the bitterness grew between these two strong men. O'Malley thought he had Rickey trapped, that no one would wish to buy Rickey's one-fourth share while O'Malley had control of the other fifty percent. Dearie Mulvey's share was not for sale.

Rickey was anxious to get out; O'Malley was fighting to get complete control of the club. Rickey offered O'Malley his share for one million dollars. O'Malley turned the offer down. He felt no one would pay that kind of money for a one-fourth share of the stock in an enterprise in the midst of conflict. What O'Malley didn't know was that Rickey had an ace in the hole. His longtime friend John Galbreath, who owned the Pittsburgh Pirates, introduced Rickey to William Zeckendorf, a wealthy real estate man. Zeckendorf signed a contract with Rickey to buy his one-fourth share for $1,050,000—

the million to go to Rickey and the $50,000 to go to Zeckendorf should O'Malley meet the price.

O'Malley was understandably livid. The price was high, but that was it. He wanted control of the Dodgers and he wanted Rickey out.

Much as I love the Rickeys, I couldn't help feeling a little sorry for O'Malley. How his pride must have been hurt—not that he wouldn't have done the same thing if he had just thought of it first.

Mr. Rickey went from the Dodgers to be general manager for John Galbreath's Pittsburgh Pirates. I never saw my dear friends again. I still miss them. The ties between my husband and Rickey were long and deep. Although it was MacPhail who had brought Red to Brooklyn, he had stayed on after MacPhail enlisted in the Army and Rickey had become general manager. Their fondness for each other was instant, and grew with the eight years they worked together. It extended to the two families. Sarah and I shared many Sunday afternoons with Mrs. Rickey and her family in her box.

When the bitter parting between O'Malley and Rickey came to its explosive end, Red's contract had one year to run. It was no secret that Red was Mr. Rickey's man. Everyone knew that it was not only a professional relationship, but also a close personal friendship of eight years standing. O'Malley had every reason to feel that Red gave his loyalty first to Rickey. This was why, shortly after Rickey left, Red went to O'Malley and said that his present contract had a full year to run, but that if O'Malley felt he would be more comfortable having a man of his own choosing broadcasting the games, he would be glad to tear up his contract. Mr. O'Malley declined most graciously, saying, "Oh, no, I want you broadcasting my games." Nevertheless, the idea persisted that Red was somehow still "Rickey's man."

Except for spring training, I had little contact with the ball club. We were living in Scarborough-on-the-Hudson. An hour-long ride on the commuting train into Grand Central, followed by another long subway ride to Ebbets Field, was just too much of a hassle, even though we could ride home in the car with Red. I only went to Sunday games, when Sarah could go along. We often sat in Mrs. O'Malley's box as her guests. She had some sort of throat surgery when she was young, a tracheotomy I would guess, and spoke in almost a whisper. It was difficult to understand her, but we both tried, and with the help of some sign language and a bit of writing we grew to be friends. She was one of the bravest and gentlest people I have ever known.

When Red was inducted into the Baseball Hall of Fame at Cooperstown in 1978, Peter O'Malley, Walter's son and now president of the Dodgers, invited Red to come to Los Angeles and throw out the first ball before a National League championship game. I was invited to come along. We sat in Peter's box and Mrs. O'Malley came in a wheelchair with an attendant and stayed for an inning or two. She died not long after. Walter died a year later at the Mayo Clinic.

In the years I knew and saw Walter and Mrs. O'Malley, I never once saw him impatient. He was always gentle, soft-spoken, and attentive. His loving, caring way was always there. I saw Walter O'Malley mostly at spring training time, when we were all together at Vero Beach. I found him most pleasant, always gracious and polite. I do not know how he was when he was working with the team, but that was none of my business.

I still remember his St. Patrick's Day parties. They were for staff and friends and family, and they were great.

No, I was not a fan, but I found much to admire and respect and, yes, like in Walter O'Malley.

A few days before Christmas in 1950 my mother suffered what was to be a fatal accident. She was struck by a car as she walked, with the traffic light green, across a busy downtown intersection, on her way home from Cohen's Department Store. Her arms were filled with presents for her family. The three of us spent the holiday in Jacksonville, Florida, watching Mother lie in a coma. There was brain surgery, and for a few hours we hoped for some response. There was none.

Red had to leave for his assignment to broadcast the Rose Bowl game in California. I went back to Scarborough so that Sarah would be there when school started after the Christmas break. Mother died February 24, 1951, two long months after she had been hit. I spent the agony of her two-month coma shuttling by plane between New York and Jacksonville.

In those eight weeks before she died the young man who had hit her never once called to inquire about her. We soon learned that the car he was driving belonged to his brother, a policeman on the Jacksonville force, and that the car was not insured.

The bittersweet relationship of mother and daughter has been going on since Eve bore her first female child. The theme is universal. Just this past year, *Terms of Endearment*, the movie starring Shirley MacLaine and Debra Winger, won the Oscar for best picture; the story deals with the age-old warring-loving relationship between mother and daughter.

I grew up sensing there was no love between my mother and her mother, but that Mother had loved her grandmother Minerva. Nothing was spelled out in words, but the silence was eloquent. Even after Mother remarried and we lived only two blocks away from Dannie's cottage, I cannot recall a single time that Dannie was in my stepfather's home. I do not think the omission was of his doing. My brother and I were routinely sent across town on Sunday afternoons to visit Grandma Scarborough, my father's mother. My stepfather encouraged the visits.

When World War II broke out, Mother and my brother were living in a small residential hotel in Jacksonville, Florida. It was an arrangement that suited her perfectly. She had no household responsibilities, there were restaurants nearby, and other people living in the hotel with whom to play bridge, a game at which she was expert. I think it may have been the happiest time of her life.

By the time my brother, who was in the Army Air Corps, was sent overseas to England, we were living in the house which we had built in Scarsdale. It was large, there was plenty of room, and we invited Mother to come and live with us. As long as I was able to have satisfactory domestic help, things went smoothly. That didn't last long. There were too many good jobs in the various defense plants.

Sarah was only four at the time of the attack on Pearl Harbor, and my sole freedom from the house depended entirely on Mother's cooperation, which was grudgingly given and within well-understood restrictions. She would not prepare the simplest sort of meal, and she would take no responsibility for any young friend to come and play with Sarah.

I do not wish to sound too harsh. As I write now I can understand better. How could she give what she had never received? I had hoped it would be a happy time for her. If it was, she never told me. I am a verbal person. I would have liked a warm, relaxed relationship. It never happened. I could not break down the silence she brought with her.

With Sarah things were different. Mother loved her granddaughter. They spent many afternoons together in Mother's room listening on radio to the soap operas. Sarah also learned to play solitaire and rummy. They obviously enjoyed each other's company. On our isolated two acres Sarah had no friends within walking distance for young children. Our allotted two gallons of gasoline per week were scarcely enough to get Sarah to school. Her father rode a bicycle to and from the station to catch the commuting train into New York.

I was simply overwhelmed with the big house, the daily meals to prepare for four people, laundry, indifferent domestic help when there was any—all this, added to the constant apprehension for our two brothers, both of whom were in the European war zone almost from the beginning of hostilities. It was a hard time for everyone.

When the war in Europe was finally over and General Eisenhower came home, his return was celebrated with a big reception and banquet at the Waldorf Hotel. At the last minute the Red Cross was allotted a table and Red was invited to be present and bring me. I assumed that Mother would be pleased at my opportunity. Not so. She made it plain that she was the one who should have been invited.

She had given her son to the war effort, while my husband had remained safe at home. It was obvious that she was not going to prepare supper and look after Sarah for the evening. In desperation I called a woman in Scarsdale who had upon occasion boarded our cats and the dog when we were out of town. Bless her, she came and I went to the banquet, but I had been robbed of much of the pleasure.

The move into the apartment at 1035 Fifth Avenue in 1946 had been traumatic for Sarah. The formalized life at a private girls school in the city was completely different from the casual atmosphere which she was accustomed to in the country. She became ill, both physically and emotionally. She was afraid to go to school and begged with tears not to be taken there. I got the best professional counsel I could find. I was told she must go, no matter how difficult it was to get her there.

Mother made it increasingly obvious that she disapproved of my efforts to carry out the professional advice I had been given. I don't know what she expected me to do. The crisis came suddenly. One morning when Sarah was crying and begging not to be made to go to school because she was too ill, Mother upbraided me, saying that I was a cruel and unnatural mother who was deliberately making her child ill. Red, who heard it all, told her that she would have to go back to Jacksonville, that we could no longer live together. So Mother left us and returned to Florida to live with my brother Mat.

As for Sarah, she soon adjusted to the new environment, made new friends, and became a happy student at Spence.

Aside from the routine problem of the adolescent girl trying to establish her own identity apart from her mother, Sarah had another, more difficult one. She was the daughter of a man whose name and face were "public property." Her father was at the height of his career, and she resented being "Red Barber's daughter." This was particularly true later, when she became a student at Rollins College. It didn't help any when President Hugh McKean asked her father to be one of the speakers on the "Animated Magazine," an annual spring event at which several people well known in their respective fields were invited to be Magazine speakers.

Sarah was doing well at Rollins. She was well liked by her fellow students. Her academic grades were good and she was on the editorial board of the *Flamingo*, the college literary magazine to which she was a frequent contributor. In a very special way Rollins was hers. Her father's presence was almost an infringement on her territorial rights. Nor did it help when, several years after her graduation, Rollins gave Red an honorary doctorate. The college has a policy of not giving the degree to a recipient with a child who is an active student at Rollins.

Sarah's problem about being "Red Barber's daughter" was not resolved for her until she was thirty-five years old and had been teaching second and third grades in the heart of Harlem for nine years. She was well aware of the role Branch Rickey and Jackie Robinson had played in the struggle to break the color line in major league baseball. She had gone with us to spring training that pivotal year of 1949 when Mr. Rickey took the Dodgers to the former Naval Air Training Station at Vero Beach.

Robinson brought Mrs. Robinson and young Jackie, who was then three years old. The Rickeys had brought a granddaughter of the same age, and the two were constant playmates. We had brought our Sarah, who was twelve, and Mike Gavin, who covered the Dodgers for the New York *Journal-American*, had brought his family. The Gavins' daughter was just Sarah's age and they were most companionable. It was a relaxed, happy time for all. Spring training is the last such time for baseball families before the long hot days and nights and lonely road trips of summer begin.

With her background of her growing-up years in the world of baseball and her nine years of teaching in Harlem, it was natural that when Robinson died, Sarah would want to go to his funeral. When she reached the church she was surprised to find the entrance cordoned off by the police, and admission allowed only with credentials. She was desperate, and she identified herself as Red Barber's daugh-

ter to a police officer. He told her he could do nothing, but pointed to
Howard Cosell, who was covering the funeral for television, and
said, "I guess if anybody can get you in, he can." When Cosell became convinced she was really who she claimed to be, he took her in
to a good seat down in the front of the church. So it was not so bad
being "Red Barber's daughter" after all.

I happen to think that Sarah had more right to be present than
many of the official dignitaries who were there. From personal experience she knew the impact of Robinson's courage on the history of
race relations in the United States.

In 1966 Red offered Sarah and me a two-week tour of Scandinavia
which we accepted with delight. We had a great trip together. Sarah
was now twenty-nine and I was sixty. We were just good friends
sharing a pleasant experience. It had taken years, and much hard
work on both sides, to bring it off but it was worth it. However, I
must say, I would not go through Sarah's adolescence again, or my
own for that matter—not for all the tea in China.

A VIEW OF THE HUDSON

It was in 1950, during Branch Rickey's final season as president of the Brooklyn Dodgers, that we built our "dream house" on the Hudson River. This is the way it began. The apartment building on 1035 Fifth Avenue was sold. The new owners elected to co-op and split the large old apartments into studios and smaller units. No leases were to be renewed. My idyllic years as a New Yorker were over. Red, who has never really cared for big city apartment dwelling, wanted to move back to Westchester County. We had kept our membership at Sleepy Hollow Country Club in Scarborough during the years we lived in New York, and we began looking for land to build on in that area. Our only building experience, the house in Scarsdale, had been happy, and we were confident, even a bit cocksure, I suspect.

We found the perfect site, two acres on top of a hill overlooking the club and the Hudson where it broadens into Haverstraw Bay. Across the river rose the Palisades and High Tor. We wanted to build a contemporary house that would take advantage of the majestic view. After much research and advice we chose a well-known firm of architects who specialized in skyscrapers but who liked to "do a special house for certain clients." At the time the Brooklyn club was having great seasons, and the broadcasts of the games had a tremendous listening audience. Red's name and face were well known. He was very busy professionally and had almost no free time. He was also traveling with the club when it went on the road. By special arrangement and for a larger than usual fee the architectural firm took over all the business arrangements with the builder whom they chose. They told Red whom to pay, when to pay, and how much.

By early summer architectural plans were complete; the builder had been chosen and ground was broken for the foundation. Our lease on the apartment in town expired July 1, Sarah's school year at Spence was finished, and we moved into the main house of the

Sleepy Hollow Country Club, where we expected to live for the
months of the actual building of our house. The handsome old mansion was one of a number built along the Hudson River as summer
homes for the New York tycoons of the late 1890s and the early
1900s. The architect, we were told, was the famous Stanford White
who had been shot and killed in the Madison Square Roof Garden by
Harry K. Thaw. The latter gentleman resented White's affair with
the actress Evelyn Nesbitt, who was Thaw's wife.

The house was a beautiful three-story structure. The rooms were
huge with very high ceilings. I remember in particular the elaborately carved marble fireplaces that had been imported from Italy.
Our quarters were on the third floor. Our bedroom, a corner room,
was large enough to have part of it fitted as a sitting room. Sarah had
an adjoining bedroom and bath. Elegant but not exactly cozy. In the
fall the main house was closed, and only the golf house remained
open. It was a much smaller wooden Victorian structure with only
three bedrooms upstairs, which the three of us occupied the winter
of 1950–51. A small restaurant remained open for the convenience
of members who lived year round in the neighboring village of Scarborough. We lived at the club nearly a year. It was considerate of the
board to help us by allowing us to use the upstairs rooms while the
construction of our house continued at a tedious pace.

We expected to be in our home by late fall, but progress had been
slow. There was a delay in the arrival of the thermopane for windows, and by early winter work was practically at a standstill.
A feeling of unease began to grow. Red's questions to the architects
and the builder were met with evasive answers. The architects said
that the builder was having a problem meeting some of the sub-
contractor's bills and consequently they were holding up deliveries.
The thermopane, for instance, was needed to enclose the house and
make it possible to continue work on the interior in the bitter winter
cold. The architects advised Red to advance, through them, the
needed money to the builder. There wasn't much else he could do,
and he had no reason to question their professional judgment. Theirs
was, after all, one of the prestige firms of New York.

Red left for Miami and spring training in March and Sarah and I remained behind in New York. I watched the work on the house get slower and slower. There would be days when no one showed. By then Red, on instructions from the architects, had advanced to the builder the full amount of the contract, but it didn't seem to be doing much good. Finally, the day before Sarah and I were to leave on her spring vacation to join Red in Miami, I made a desperation call to the architects. I told them I felt the builder was no longer arriving for work. I was met with a curt rejoinder that it was really none of my business, that they were in charge. So Sarah and I left the next morning by train to join Red in Miami. I was apprehensive, but still glad to leave the nightmare behind, no matter what the outcome.

Red met us at the station with the exciting news that we were taking the afternoon boat for Havana and a weekend vacation. We were so happy to be together again with all problems left behind in the United States. The boat was crowded. The American association of black morticians was holding its national convention in Havana, and they were happy and on holiday, too. There was laughter and music and spirited dancing. We enjoyed the merriment and the three days we had in Cuba. It was well we did. When Red checked in at the hotel desk in Miami he was greeted with, "Where have you been? New York has been calling frantically for three days!" Red soon got the bleak news. The builder had gone broke, left the country, disappeared, and the sub-contractors were howling for blood. There was nothing to do but return to New York and try to put the pieces back together. We had a three-quarters finished house and no builder. Red had to become legal contractor and builder, a role for which he certainly had no training. He put up his life insurance for collateral and borrowed the money from his bank to finish the job.

Lou Crandall, president of Fuller Construction Company, our good friend whom we had gotten to know in Ciudad Trujillo, came to the rescue. He sent one of his foremen and a crew to finish the house to the point that we could move in. I don't know what would have happened without his help. The support in the basement for the large living and dining area had to be completely rebraced. Doors

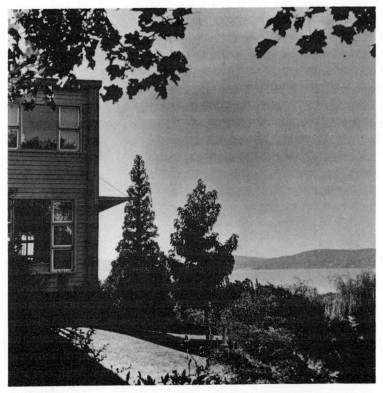

The house on the Hudson—*photo by Tony Venti.*

had to be rehung. The plumbing in the master bath had to be redone. When we moved in, the toilet bowl for the master bath was
sitting in the dressing room passage between the bedroom and the
bathroom. It was a mess. We were years getting all the bad work-
manship straightened out. A crack developed in the fireplace wall in
the living room, and a whole side of the wall had to be redone.

When the weather turned cold that first fall we discovered that we
had a schizophrenic furnace. It cut off when the outside temperature
went down. When the temperature rose, the furnace promptly came
on. The thermostat had been incorrectly hooked up. It was fixed,

and we breathed a sigh of relief. Too soon. Christmas Eve, I remember, while we were opening the last cards, the furnace simply quit. We put on extra sweaters, went into the kitchen, turned on the oven, and left the stove door open. Between the fireplaces in the living room, master bedroom, and library we survived. Finally, in desperation, Red called Bill DuBray, our nice young plumber. He left his Christmas Eve, came over, and manually got the furnace going. On December 26, we left for Miami and the Orange Bowl game on New Year's Day. Red instructed Alex Hunter, a Westchester County builder who had done much corrective work for us, to rip out the control system and replace it with a new one by a different manufacturer while we were in Miami. We had no more trouble. About two years after we broke ground, the house was finally straightened out and at last comfortable to live in. I have heard it said that "into every life some rain must fall," but did Fate, or was it the Furies, have to send a hurricane?

Once the house in Scarborough was finally finished and occupied, I turned my efforts to becoming a suburban housewife, a role to which I was suited neither by temperament nor past experience. Life in the commuting villages in Westchester County and on Long Island revolved around the weekend. At least it did in the days when I was trying to adjust; I don't know how it is today, some thirty years later, but my guess is that it continues much the same. The men did their Monday-through-Friday bit in the city, while their wives chauffeured children to school and afternoon activities. Their free time was during the school hours. Bridge games and luncheons were popular. I cared little for either. Social events on week nights were almost nonexistent; that commuting train into the city leaves mighty early in the morning. On weekends it was different. There were dinner parties, Saturday night dances at the club, and brunches on Sundays. Early retirement on Sunday evening was the pattern. Monday morning and the commuting train brought back reality.

Red was often traveling with the ball club or out of town on football assignments. He was away from home, by a conservative estimate, half of the time. By the 1950s baseball had become—Mondays through Fridays—almost entirely a nighttime game. On Saturdays and Sundays the games were played in the afternoon, but as the season wore on there were many Sunday doubleheaders. I have often said I was for all practical purposes a widow, but one without the privileges of that estate.

I was out of step.

As I think back and write of those days the words keep coming into my mind, "out of step" and "lonely." I was often lonely and alone. Red was gone much of the time, and by then Sarah was away at prep school and college. I was not resentful or bitter. I understood the rules. Red was at the peak of his career as a broadcaster, and that had to come first. While there were many lonely days and nights there were also times of great excitement and wonderful experiences that would not have come to me except for my husband's singular way of earning a living.

Years later when Mr. and Mrs. Curt Gowdy were in our home on Key Biscayne for an evening, Jerre and I talked about the similarity of our lives. Their children were teenagers, and she felt they needed more of their father's company. I understood too well. Sarah had needed more of her father in those difficult adolescent years, and I certainly needed his comforting support. Jerre said to me, "I am so lonely." I remember my reply to her: "You must let him have his career." For me there was no other way.

My experiment at trying to fit into the suburban routine was short-lived. I found my compensation in other ways. There was one special friendship that began shortly after we moved to Scarborough, while we were still living at the country club. It came through Saint Mary's, the little Episcopal church situated on the grounds of Sleepy Hollow Country Club. Saint Mary's parish is an old one, having been founded in 1839. For several years the congregation worshipped in a one-room district school. By the late 1840s or early 1850s the church had been built. It is, insofar as possible, a duplication of the north aisle chapel of the thirteenth-century Saint Mary's Church in Yorkshire, England. It is built of the native gray granite, and is one of the

At home in the living room of the house on the Hudson: Sarah, Beau, Red, and Lylah.

finest examples of the English Gothic style in America. The stained glass windows are the work of John Bolton, who came from England and established one of the earliest stained glass studios in this country at Pelham in Westchester County. They are beautiful.

We became members of the parish shortly after we moved to Scarborough in 1950. I felt especially drawn, since my maiden name is Scarborough and family tradition says that the first Scarboroughs came to colonial America from the English town of that name. In 1956 when the church was completely restored, I served on the three-member committee responsible for the work. It was a labor of love.

Shortly after we moved to Scarborough, Mrs. Baldwin, the wife of the rector, invited me to go with her to a women's auxiliary luncheon meeting in nearby Bronxville. I was anxious to meet people who would be neighbors in what was now my new hometown. I accepted.

When I arrived at the rectory she introduced me to Peggy Bloch, who was to drive us to the meeting.

When I met Peggy I was in my early forties and she was just a few years younger. She was pretty, a tall slender woman with brown hair and big brown eyes. When she spoke her voice was soft and Southern, the accent I had grown up with. Before the day was over we found out how much more we had in common. She too had a daughter, a year older than my Sarah. Our family backgrounds and upbringings were similar. Since she was married to a man almost thirty years her senior who was not in robust health, her social activities too were curtailed.

A few days after we met, Peggy invited Red and me to come to dinner at Woodlands. She had told us there would be a sign with the name Bloch telling us where to turn off the road. We turned but we drove and drove, past a cabin seen through the woods and a lake with an island in the center and a footbridge leading to a gazebo. We began to feel that somehow we had gotten lost, but it was summer and there was still twilight so we decided to drive a little further. Finally we came to the house. It was of simple Georgian lines, sitting in beautifully kept grounds, charming, but not in the least ostentatious. What Peggy had neglected to tell us was that Woodlands sat in the midst of ninety-eight acres of prime Westchester County land. I could not know that summer night that Woodlands was to become for me, for many years, almost a second home.

Harold Bloch, the night we met, did seem old to me. I am amused as I write to realize that he must have been younger than I am now. I know he celebrated his seventieth birthday not long after we met. I liked him from the first meeting. Harold had a sharp tongue and very definite opinions, but he was sophisticated and charming and slowly we grew to be friends. I was with Peggy when he died. She is still my close friend. We are really more like sisters.

Peggy was helpful in so many ways those first days of adjustment. It was she who told me that Sarah must not appear at the first fall dancing class at the country club in her short party dress and sox, but in silk stockings and a long dress. Her advice was most fortu-

nate. Sarah was having trouble enough getting used to the Briarcliff
public school, which was so different from Spence in New York,
without showing up at dancing class differently dressed; such mis-
takes are catastrophic when one is thirteen years old. A year later
Sarah joined my friend's daughter, also Peggy, at the Masters School
in Dobbs Ferry, where she felt much more at home.

Peggy was the parish contact with Youth Consultation Service, a
social service of the Episcopal Church in New York State. Harold
was not well, and was impatient with the time the work took her
away from Woodlands and him. She asked me if I would take her
place. I did, and it gave meaning and purpose to what otherwise
could have been many lonely hours. I think I am a more compassion-
ate person because of my work with Youth Consultation Service.
Certainly I am less judgmental. I am very fond of young adults and
get along well with them.

I also renewed my acquaintance with Harry Crowley, the painter
and piano teacher from whom I had taken a few piano lessons in the
years we lived in Scarsdale. That experience certainly didn't make
me even a Sunday pianist, but it did improve my ear and teach me to
enjoy music more fully. (How many happy evenings my husband
and I spend in our home here in Tallahassee listening to records of
classical music.) In the intervening years Harry had become a successful painter in oils with several one-man shows in New York City
to his credit. We have a number of his paintings which we bought
over the years.

Harry, who died in 1979, was a person of contradictions. His
mother was a Vermont Yankee, a Protestant whom he obviously
loved. His father, in contrast, was an Irish Roman Catholic whom he
did not love. I once heard Harry say, "He killed my mother with a
hard life and too much childbearing." At the time we knew Harry he
was an agnostic, and had been, I would imagine, most of his life. His
nativity painting says it all. The background is the barren winter
hills of the Judean landscape near Bethlehem, which we saw when
we were there, but it is also the low mountains in the farming country of Vermont where Harry grew up. The stable, where the mother

and child are, is a shed protected from the elements by the most rudimentary of canopies. The people standing nearby have not come to praise. Their faces are hard, cynical, unbelieving. There are no wise men bearing gifts. Only one person, a small child, kneels at the foot of the crib. He holds in his hands a gift of a few flowers, but his face is bright with love. He believes. By his side a cat watches. I think it may well be the best thing Harry painted. It never fails to move me. Every Christmas, when we hang his Nativity for the season, the two Harrys come back into our house for a few days.

This second time in Westchester County, in Scarborough, I did not try again to play the piano, but I did paint with Harry. Once a week I had a most informal lesson. I painted along with him, and he showed me what was good and what wasn't. He made me do some drawing exercises, which I am not very good at and did not enjoy, but I did enjoy the painting very much. I converted the room intended for a sleep-in maid into a studio and painted for hours every day. I remember one Sunday after Red left for Yankee Stadium and a doubleheader, I was reading the *New York Times* on a lounge in the garden. I turned to the travel section and there was a small black-and-white underwater photograph illustrating an article on snorkeling in the waters off Bermuda. I had been in Bermuda twice, and had even tried my hand at snorkeling. I recalled well the beauty of that underwater world and the fishes in it. I went into the studio and began to paint. I was not aware of the passing of time. Finally I was satisfied, I had done my best. I became aware of Red standing in the doorway. I don't know how long he had been there, but it was dark outside. He had broadcast a doubleheader since I had started painting. I had not even stopped for lunch. There was no preparation for supper. I had entirely forgotten. Red was amused and patient. Fortunately, he never wanted anything more than a light supper after a doubleheader. He was too tired to eat much. We made a drink and nibbled on crackers and cheese. It was midnight by the time we got to bed, both of us tired but with a sense of accomplishment. It had been a good day.

THE OLD WORLD WAS NEW

There was another escape hatch from the tedium of the long days and nights alone in the big, empty house. It became an established custom with Red and me to spend what free time he had in travel. Red had been in Europe, but, except for the islands in the Caribbean, I had never been outside the continental United States.

After Sarah became a boarding student at the Masters School and I was free of my day-by-day responsibility for her care, I was able to make my first trip to Europe. Since we had to travel in the late winter and early spring because of Red's working schedule, we elected to go only to Italy and Spain. We had a better chance of good weather in those countries. The flight over—it was in the pre-jet era—was a long one, and at night. Seated across the aisle from us were a man and his wife who were traveling with their two Siamese cats in a cage. He was employed in the State Department, and they were being transferred to a new assignment. The cats howled all night. If you have ever had any contact with Siamese cats you know what that cry is like. We landed in Paris in time for breakfast. We had an hour or so to wait in the airport and then flew on to Rome. Everyone was relieved when the cat fanciers and their charges did not continue on the flight.

The travel agent at American Express who arranged our tour had owned a department store in Brooklyn and had become a fan of the Dodgers and Red's broadcasts of the games. He was also a personal friend of Angelo Bettoja, the Italian industrialist who owned a chain of hotels in Italy. We had met Mr. and Mrs. Bettoja at a cocktail party our American Express friend gave for them when they were on a visit to New York. Bettoja had said that when we came to Rome we would have to stay at his hotel, the Mediterraneo. We knew that those arrangements had been made, but we did not know until we were paged over the loudspeaker in the airport that his car and chauffeur were waiting to drive us into the city. Dino, a sort of gen-

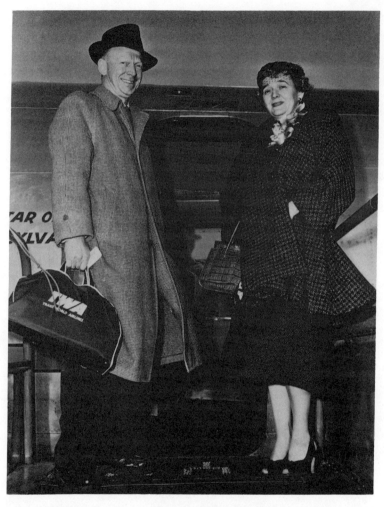
Ready to leave on our first pleasure trip to Italy and Spain.

eral factotum of the Bettojas, and the car were placed at our disposal for our stay in Rome. He had been instructed, instead of driving the fast highway into town, to take us on the ancient Appian Way. How wonderful—catapulted in a few seconds from the modern glassy airport across the centuries to the same cobblestones on which the Roman legions marched into the city.

Our room turned out to be a penthouse suite with a terrace and a lovely view of the city. There were a vase of yellow roses, a bottle of Scotch, and a bowl of ice waiting. Ours was a royal welcome to the Eternal City.

In our haste to savor the joys of travel, Red had purchased tickets to Massenet's *Manon*, which was being performed that night at the Rome Opera House. We were in for an evening of surprises. First, the auditorium was small, or so it seemed in comparison with the Met in New York City. The setting was charming, but our seats were certainly not designed primarily for comfort. After what felt like hours to two tired travelers the curtains parted and the music began—we were learning about the Roman concept of time. I am sure the performance was superb, but I dozed through most of it. Red, who is more knowledgeable about opera than I, did a bit better.

During our ten-day stay in Italy we lived in a perpetual state of excitement. We did, with gusto, all the things that tourists do. We took the bus trip from Rome to Florence. We drove through the hilly, soft Umbrian countryside and stopped at St. Francis' town of Assisi for lunch. We arrived in Florence at dusk. I remember the heavy bicycle traffic and how carefully our bus made its way. We stayed at the elegant Excelsior on the banks of the Arno just across the square from the equally elegant Grand Hotel. Rome is eternal but Florence was, to me on my first visit, a city of endless delight. We went to the Uffizi Gallery and the Pitti Palace. We saw beautiful paintings that I had known only from photographs in art books as I was growing up. We shopped on the Ponte Vecchio, and I bought silver bracelets for friends back home.

I have a weakness for beautiful shoes. My aunt Ouida's husband, the one who was a doctor, once said that his ambition was to make enough money to buy the Watts women (my mother, Aunt Ouida, and me) all the shoes they wanted. What fun I had in the Ferragamo shop.

We also researched the restaurants. There was the evening, I think it was at Sabatino's, that I met my first octopus looking at me face to face on my antipasto plate. I was hesitant, but I was not going to be stared down by a many-armed mollusk. It was, of course, delicious. Another day we went north of Florence to Fiesole, a drive of about a half-hour, for lunch. We had an artichoke omelet, another "first." After lunch I inquired from our waiter the location of the restroom. By then I was quite accustomed to the European coeducational facility, but I had a different one coming. He pointed to a door opening onto a long balcony. I entered the room at the balcony's end, which was sort of cantilevered out over the top of the hill. There lay, as I saw through a large glass window, a magnificent view of the city of Florence. I have often wondered how many tourists discovered by chance, as I did, that "water closet with a view." When Red asked me, "What kept you so long?" all I could say was, "Go see for yourself."

The spring of 1953 was a cold one for Italy. When we returned from Florence, Rome was in the grip of an influenza epidemic. Pope Pius XII was ill in his palace in the Vatican, and Red followed suit in our penthouse suite in the Mediterraneo Hotel. Our planned trip to Naples, Sorrento, and Capri was cancelled. The remainder of our Italian holiday was spent, at a more leisurely pace, in Rome.

Red and I saw the Colosseum twice, first in the daylight, then, realizing there was a full moon, we went back at night and stood there alone except for the ubiquitous cats of Rome. Mr. Bettoja's Dino drove us to see Ostia Antica, the ancient port of Rome, which was then still in the process of excavation and restoration. The sandy beach was a pale gray, not at all like the white beaches of our Atlantic seaboard.

Our Italian adventure closed with luncheon as the guests of Mr. and Mrs. Bettoja at their apartment in a beautiful residential section of Rome. The next day, when Red went to the desk to pay our bill and leave for the airport and our flight to Spain he was told, "There is no charge." We were overwhelmed.

I do not know why, but from my early childhood Spain had been for me a place of mystery filled with fairies, castles, Moors, and gypsies. To be there conjured up for me all the people and things of the fairytales I had read so avidly as a child. The approach by plane was all I could have asked for—appropriate, dramatic. I was even pleased that we landed in Madrid at night.

Our room at the Ritz was large, with a pleasant sitting area in a bay window with a view of the Plaza de la Lealtad. The bathroom was also large and the plumbing was elegant but unpredictable. The water storage for the toilet was in a tank near the ceiling. That we had seen before, but this one had a personality of its own. The chain did not always produce a flushing. There was one instance when it did not work. We had ordered a bottle of wine which had arrived in a large silver bucket filled with ice. Fortunately, the bucket was still in the room. Red filled it with water from the tub and poured it in the toilet. The crisis was solved for the moment. Red reported to the desk and was assured the situation "would be corrected immediately." Nothing had happened when we went out for the evening, but when we returned late, quite a while after midnight, there was the repair man busily at work in the bathroom. Having learned about the Spanish "mañana," we did not dare ask him to return the next morning. It made for a late evening even by Spanish custom.

The Prado Museum was nearby, filled with the masterpieces of the great Spanish painters—Murillo, Goya, El Greco. I suppose if I were asked to choose one painter above all others it would have to be El Greco. A highlight of our stay in Spain was, for me, the day we spent in Toledo. We left Madrid early in the morning and drove through the sparsely settled arid country. We passed occasional ancient castles sitting on top of their hills. This was February, and it was bitter cold. I could see poor Don Quixote tilting at the windmills which dotted the barren landscape. It was so cold that our guide insisted we stop at a roadside tavern, I suppose it was, and have a small glass of Spanish brandy. This was another first for me—brandy in the middle of the morning. I would not recommend it as a usual sight-seeing procedure, but it did warm us a bit. We stood outside, looked far down to the Tagus River and across to Toledo. It all looked like a painting by El Greco. Toledo is an ancient city, and the Roman and Moorish influence was everywhere. We had luncheon at a little inn inside the city walls, and I ordered perdice, a small quail-like bird, the "specialty of the house." Never mind that I had to pay for it with traveler's disease the next day in Madrid.

The Spain that we saw in 1953 was a land of uneasy truce. One felt the tension of Franco's dictatorship everywhere. The Spanish people we met were guarded. This was especially true of our guide and driver. He was an attractive man, perhaps in his early forties, who had worked in his youth in the British merchant marine. He spoke excellent English. He had fought on the losing side in the Spanish Civil War and had been active in the siege of Madrid. Carlos, I think his name was, was knowledgeable, obliging, and most polite, but he had one peculiar quirk. I could not figure why. He never spoke di-rectly to my husband. He would say, "Madame, tell your husband," or "Madame, ask your husband." Something to do with Spanish "macho," perhaps?

We were in Madrid on Sunday and went in the morning to a little Anglican church in a residential section. We were told that it was the only Protestant church in all of Roman Catholic Madrid. The rectory and church, hardly more than a chapel, were inside a wall. Two soldiers stood at attention outside the entrance. When we left after the service, which had been attended by only a handful of people, the two soldiers were still on guard. When we asked, "Why were the soldiers there?" we were told, "For your protection."

After church services we drove out to El Escorial, the summer palace of King Philip II, for another of those extended Spanish mid-day meals. While we were sightseeing after the luncheon we came upon a chapel where a vesper service was in progress. The chanting was beautiful, and we stood in the back and listened for a while. I turned to Carlos and started to speak. He quickly put his finger to his lips. I got the warning and remained quiet. After we were alone in the car, Carlos explained, "Be careful what you say in a public building, they are listening everywhere." I didn't ask who "they" were.

When the time came for the flight to Seville and southern Spain, I had not recovered entirely from my bout with the Toledo perdice and was feeling a little rocky. Carlos, who took such good care of me and all but ignored Red, insisted as he was bidding us goodbye that I go into the airport restaurant and have a cup of tea "to settle my stomach." While we were sitting there and I was trying to get down the tea and gather my courage for the flight two young men in flight officers' uniforms and carrying swagger sticks came in. They sat at the nearby bar and both ordered brandy. I assumed that they had finished their tour of duty and were enjoying a little relaxation. The plane was small, and we were no more than settled in our seats when our two companions of the restaurant, swagger sticks and all, walked down the aisle and disappeared into the cockpit—our pilot and co-pilot! We took off almost immediately. The flight was short and smooth, but the landing was a little unusual. It was easy, no bumps, but after the plane landed we just taxied straight into a hangar and the plane was parked for the night. We sat and waited until the two pilots left the plane. Passengers then scrambled off as best they could.

Our reservation was in the beautiful Alfonso XIII Hotel. Our room looked like something you might find in the Spanish wing of a museum. It was spacious, rich, and there was lots of red velvet at the windows and on the beds. The surrounding gardens were in bloom with spring flowers, so welcome after the cold winter of northern Spain.

Francesco, our guide for southern Spain, was quite different from Carlos. To begin with, he didn't look Spanish. We soon found out why. His mother was Scotch; she had come to Spain as a tourist with a group of students, had fallen in love with their guide, married him, and stayed in Spain. Francesco looked like his Scotch mother, but in temperament he was very much his father's child. He was a conventional and completely Spanish male in his emotional responses.

I had been impressed in Madrid, and in the other villages and towns we visited, by the large number of women one saw in black clothing. Some were in temporary mourning perhaps for fathers or brothers, but most of them were widows. We had been told that for them the black was permanent. It defined their social status. Once I asked Francesco, "But when they remarry, don't they come out of mourning?" He replied, "Spanish men don't marry them." "Why not?" I asked. "Because they are used women." It was not said unkindly, just a statement of fact.

Red and I had planned to go to a bullfight—not that we expected to enjoy it, but since my husband's profession was sports broadcasting, it was important to observe the national sport of the country we were visiting. Soccer was more popular, but the bullrings were always filled, and the colorful bullfight was the traditional ancient sport. However, we were there during the period of Lent and the bullfight season does not open until Easter. Our only opportunity, which our guide found for us, was a festival, a charity affair. It was being held for the benefit of the hospital at Ecija, a small town some ninety odd miles northeast of Seville. Eight bullfights were included in the festivities. Four were to be performed by famous matadors, the others by novices. Everything—the bulls, the music of the band, the skills of the matadors—was to be donated for the benefit of the hospital.

When we took our seats in the arena and looked around at the Sunday crowd I was amazed at the number of people who had brought their small children—some looked no more than three or four years old—to witness the spectacle. It was not a pretty one.

As the afternoon wore on it became a bloody business. The established matadors were skillful, but the novices were not, and the bulls and horses took a fearful punishment. One humiliated novice could not "dispatch" his bull and finally called for help from a more experienced professional. Another fighter who had been particularly skillful and received thunderous applause, cut off an ear from the bull and threw it into the crowd. It landed near where we were sitting, and Francesco retrieved it. He offered it to me, a sort of testing of me, I think. I declined with as much composure as I could muster, but my stomach was churning. We did not stay for the entire program. We had seen enough.

All the drive back to Seville I kept thinking about the debasing cruelty of the bullfight and what it said about the paradoxical character of the Spanish people. I was pretty judgmental and superior. Then I thought about the popularity of prize fighting in my own country. In my imagination I heard again the roar of an American crowd when the blood begins to flow and the knockout becomes imminent. It put my thoughts in perspective.

Red and I both wanted to include the Moorish city of Granada in our Spanish holiday. I had read Washington Irving's *Tales of the Alhambra* in high school and had visited Sunnyside, his charming Victorian home in nearby Tarrytown, after we moved to Scarborough on the Hudson River.

The drive from Seville to Granada took us through sparsely settled, sometimes mountainous country. There were occasional Andalusian villages of whitewashed houses with their colorful red tile roofs, but most of the time we drove through miles of olive groves. There was very little traffic. We passed an occasional peasant riding his burro, but we met almost no automobiles. The Spain we saw in 1953, outside of the cities, was still isolated from modern Europe.

In Granada we stayed at a small hotel at the end of a narrow road, on top of a hill. Our room was a large corner one, with a balcony hung over the side of the side of the hill and a view of the Sierra Nevada range in the far distance. After dinner, late in the Spanish style, a troupe of gypsies came up from their caves and entertained the guests of the hotel. They danced the wild gypsy dances and sang the wailing laments of their people. Late in the night, long after we had retired, I was wakened by the sound of voices coming through the doors of our balcony. I stepped out. The moon was full and I saw going down the hill, on a narrow dirt road, our entertainers of the evening. They were singing again, but this time it was for themselves and to themselves. It was eerie and very beautiful. I stood alone on the balcony until dawn came and broke the spell.

From Granada we drove to Gibraltar where we waited a couple of days for our ship, the *Independence*, which was to take us home. Edward R. Murrow had given Red a letter of introduction to the governor-general of Gibraltar, whom Murrow had known during his World War II years in England. We presented ourselves at the governor's office. After a "proper" wait he appeared. He was pleasant in a reserved British sort of way. He told us the wife of the Lord of the Admiralty was a houseguest and that he and his wife were taking her on a tour of the Rock. He suggested that we follow them in our car. The tour was thorough. It even included one of the numerous tunnels that honeycombed the mountain. We visited the apes; they were friendly and well fed. A Spanish legend has it that when the apes leave the Rock the English will follow. Neither group gave any indication of leaving when we were there.

We returned to the hotel for an early supper and retirement in preparation for a 4:00 A.M. wake-up call. We dressed—no breakfast, no sign of life at the hotel—and took a taxi to the dock to wait for our ship. We were the only passengers to board. The *Independence* was late, and we waited some two hours in the cold and dark on the dock. Finally, the little boat arrived from the ship and picked us up, and we made the trip across the dark choppy waters to the ship's steps. We were taken straight to our lovely quarters on the sun deck. Our room steward arrived immediately with very hot coffee and rolls. He was obviously accustomed to the procedure at Gibraltar. It was the most welcome cup of coffee I've ever had.

My first trip to Europe was over and my first voyage on a transatlantic liner had begun. How sad that our twentieth-century rush to get from here to there in the fewest possible hours has spelled the death of that beautiful mode of travel.

I am fortunate. Since then we have enjoyed many other great trips, and seen many places. Space will not permit their retelling here. I have been on all the continents of our globe except Australia, but no other journey has held quite the magic of that first trip abroad.

There is one other trip, however, that I want to tell about. It was made not with Red but with my daughter Sarah. I had kept in touch with an old friend of my convent school days, Louise Holt, through the years when she visited New York and during spring training when the Yankees were in St. Petersburg, where she lives. Louise is a practicing Roman Catholic and has friends among the church hierarchy. When she learned that Sarah and I were planning a European trip and would be in Rome for several days, she offered to see what she could do about an audience with Pope Pius XII. I was delighted. It would mean much to me, and I was anxious for Sarah to have that unique experience.

At the time, Sarah was in college. Rollins was on the trimester system, and she had completed her third-year academic requirements by the spring break. Her father cashed in the college insurance policy he had taken out when she was born and gave the money to the two of us for a seven-week trip to Europe.

We were in Italy, France, Germany, and Portugal. We even squeezed in a boat ride on the Rhine and a few days in England and Scotland. It was, on the whole, a pleasant trip. We are both avid travelers and the few rough spots were peacefully negotiated. Sarah was twenty and I was fifty-one. We were both growing up. We were becoming congenial friends.

When I packed for the trip I included two mantillas I had bought in Seville on an earlier trip. I knew, provided we were fortunate and the audience came through, that they were necessary for head covering. As soon as we were settled in our room at the Hotel Flora, across from the Borghese Gardens, I contacted Louise's friend. He was an American priest attached to the Curia, the organization that aids the pope in the administration and government of the worldwide Roman

Lylah and Sarah in Venice. St. Mark's in the background.

Catholic Church. He had been living in Rome for many years and had been a student there. He arrived wearing the customary black cassock and the wide-brimmed black clerical hat which I was to see often in Italy. Later, he told me how he hated to wear the required "petticoats" on the street. The young, attractive, pleasant priest explained that, as I knew, the pope was quite elderly and had not been well lately. He would do his best, but I should not be too hopeful. I was to stay in touch.

Since things seemed so uncertain, Sarah and I decided to take our planned trip down to Sorrento and Capri. Several days later when we returned from our excursion, happy but tired, there was a message from our friend. It was late in the evening, but we forgot our fatigue on being informed that there would be an audience the next morning. We had to be at the Vatican by 7:00 A.M. We made it, but with only a few moments to spare. We were met inside the papal residence by two members of the Swiss Guard, the personal guard to the popes since the 1500s. We were told it was late. We must hurry. We must remain silent.

I still remember the clatter made by our leather heels as we ran down the long marble-floored corridor. Out of breath we finally reached the room where the other people were gathered. It was a small audience, maybe twenty in all. There were several nuns, a young woman in a wheelchair, a family including several teenaged children, and a group of young boys in what appeared to be school uniforms. The Barbers and several middle-aged people completed the group. We were instructed to kneel when presented.

We waited, maybe five minutes, then Pope Pius XII entered. He was indeed frail and was assisted on either side by attendants. I had expected elaborate vestments, but instead he wore a simple white cassock with slippers to match. His face was thin, almost to the point of asceticism. His eyes were alive and piercing. I remember how beautiful his hands were, large and slender. In appearance he might have been one of El Greco's saints. He visited with each group, in their own language. That was how I discovered the family group was from the United States. The pope's English was flawless.

Fortunately Sarah and I were near the last group visited, so that by the time he reached us we had been able to observe the proper protocol and could behave accordingly. Being of the Anglican communion we were accustomed to ritual. We liked it. My college-student daughter was impressed and moved. Certainly I was. I felt the strength and authority of a great force.

I got out of Lake City.

Learning to talk to American troops
overseas.

Waiting for the airplane to take us to the U.S. Strategic Air
Command bases in the Mediterranean.

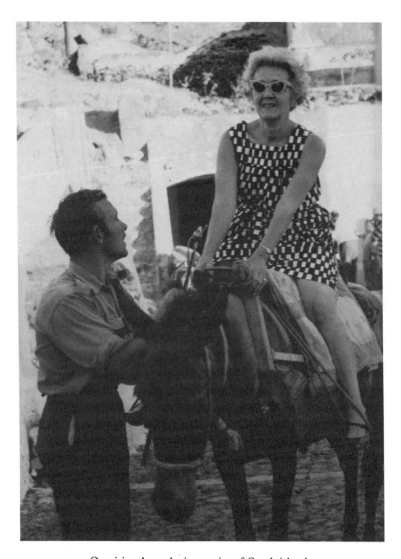

On visit ashore during cruise of Greek islands.

Arriving at Kyushu, Japan, on U.S.O. tour of Pacific.

THE MOVE TO THE YANKEES

On our first trip to Spain together, Red had bought himself a boina, a Basque-type beret. The boina was a comfort in cold northern Spain and on deck on the voyage home. Red grew attached to it, and the boina went with us to Vero Beach for spring training in 1953. That little Basque hat proved to be a symbol of the events that led to his departure from the Brooklyn Dodgers organization.

The first day he came to practice, he wore the boina, more as a gag than anything else. Barney Stein, the club photographer, wanted a picture of the two Walters, O'Malley and Barber, together for the Dodger yearbook. He told Red to remove the cap.

It was the wrong approach. Red said, "If you want a picture, take it like I am." He did not wear the hat again that spring.

Opening day at Brooklyn was cold, and without being aware that a headpiece had become a situation he wore a conventional hat to work. Red was given a copy of the 1953 Dodger yearbook and asked to plug it on the air. There was the picture of the two Walters. Under it a caption read something to the effect that Red wore the boina in Florida, but that he wouldn't dare wear it in Brooklyn. Then and there the boina became a part of my husband's working uniform.

O'Malley reported that the sponsor, Schaefer Beer, was unhappy about the boina being worn on camera. The company associated the headpiece with wine, not beer. By this time everyone had become stubborn, and was overreacting. Finally the agency handling the Schaefer account sent down a dictum: "No boina while on camera doing commercials." They were entirely within their rights. They had bought and owned that time-space. My stubborn husband agreed—no beret during commercials. Still, he wore it on play-by-play until the weather got too warm.

The boina was not the reason Red left Brooklyn and went to the

Yankees in 1954, but it was a contributing irritant. Actually, as I
have noted before, Red was Rickey's man. After the bitterness between O'Malley and Rickey that saw Branch leave the Brooklyn organization, relations between O'Malley and Red became increasingly
strained. When the offer came from the New York Yankees, Red
took it. Fifteen fruitful years at Brooklyn were over.

A few days later Red ran into John Royal, an old friend and former
program director for NBC, walking down Fifth Avenue. Royal
laughed and said, "The Yankees, Red, don't give a damn about
what you wear on your head—all they care about is what you put
into the mike."

Even today, some thirty-one years after my husband became a
member of the Yankee organization, I still find it painful to write
about the thirteen years with the Yankees.

We had made several moves since our marriage—first from Gainesville, Florida, to Cincinnati and the Reds, then the move with Mac-
Phail to New York and the Dodgers, followed by MacPhail's enlist-
ment during World War II and our continuing years at Brooklyn
with Rickey and O'Malley. These had all been professional advance-
ments for Red and happy new experiences for me. But something
about the move to Yankee Stadium just did not seem right to me.

The offer came about in this way. Red and I were having lunch at a
table with Mr. and Mrs. Bob Carpenter, who owned the Philadelphia
Phillies. Everyone was waiting for game five of the 1953 Yankee-
Dodgers World Series. Each club had won two games. I looked up
just in time to see Dan Topping and George Weiss coming into the
dining room. Topping and Del Webb were co-owners of the Yankees,
and Weiss was general manager. Weiss came alone to our table and
asked Red if he would come over and have a word with Topping.

I had been in baseball long enough to know that group wasn't
planning to discuss the latest changes in women's fashions. I don't
remember who won the game. I could not have cared less. I knew
that my husband's future was probably being decided, but that I
would not know how or in what way until we were alone.

I suppose, in a way, that episode set the tone for my years with the Yankees. Maybe I was introduced to Weiss, but I don't remember. I felt like a "non-person."

I was distressed when I learned what Red's working schedule would be. He was the top man in the game at play-by-play broadcasting, and what the Yankees wanted him to do was fifteen-minute interviews with ballplayers before and after the games. Dizzy Dean, Joe DiMaggio, and Joe E. Brown had all had a try at doing the interviews, but none of them had been satisfactory. The pre- and postgame interview has always seemed to me to be an "iffy" effort. It cannot count on a regular, dedicated audience. Before the game begins the real fan, if he can make it, is on his way to the ball park, or else waiting for the play-by-play on the radio or television. Afterwards he has other things to do.

When my husband insisted that if he took the position he must do some play-by-play, he was assigned two-and-a-half innings a game on radio and two-and-a-half on television. It was a fair enough compromise, I suppose, but I always felt that his best talents were not fully used.

The first time I had seen Yankee Stadium was in 1941. The Dodgers and the Yankees had won their pennants and the opening game of the Series was to be played at Yankee Stadium. Red was still with the Dodgers, so my seat was in the Dodger allotment, but I can't remember who was there. All I can recall is that huge stadium, with those three tiers of seats filled with more than 60,000 people. I never got over the sense of the hugeness of the building and the mass of strangers. I did not go to many games while we were still living in Scarborough, although now and then I would take a friend who enjoyed baseball. We would ride the commuting train to 125th Street and then take a taxi to the stadium. We could ride home in style with Red in the car after the game was over.

The stadium was not the only thing about the Yankees that was big. The organization was huge. The almost "family" feeling that I had known with the Reds and Dodgers under MacPhail, Rickey, and O'Malley was missing.

My first spring training with the Yankees was in 1954 and the club
stayed at the Sorena Hotel in St. Petersburg. It wasn't a very cheer-
ful place and seemed to be filled with well-to-do elderly ladies.
George and Hazel Weiss were staying there and were pleasant. I
don't recall meeting any other Yankee personnel. I'm sure some were
there, but they never introduced themselves. I was the newcomer,
and shy.

The next two years we stayed at the Tides Hotel on Redington
Beach, where we had stayed other springs and had friends, some
even from high school days.

By 1962, the Yankee stadium had been built in the Fort Lauderdale area and the Yankees trained and played their exhibition games
there. After that, we made our own spring arrangements. I had long
since given up trying to be a member of the Yankees' closed corporation. After all, Red and I were Floridians and we had many good
friends of long years in the state.

In 1963 we moved back into the city. The uprooting was traumatic. The house had been on the market for well over a year. Now
that we had decided to go back into the city, we were anxious to get
the move done. Action in the real estate field was slow, and few
prospective buyers had seen the house. The only people who had
shown much interest were our friends Helen and Nils Lundberg,
who also lived in Scarborough. Nils was a realtor who commuted
daily into New York City.

We knew that Helen had admired the house since she first saw it at
our housewarming party. Nils loved the garden with its apple and
peach orchard, and the magnificent view of the Hudson, High Tor,
and the Ramapo Mountains across the water. It was a wonderful
setting, but Red, with his heavy schedule, had little time to enjoy it.
With Mother no longer alive and Sarah grown, teaching school in
Harlem and living in New York, the setup was much too large and
expensive for the two of us. There had been a little half-serious
banter between the two husbands with Nils saying, "Red, you drive
a hard bargain," and my husband replying, "Nils, you are tough."

The situation seemed to be at a stalemate when we left for spring training.

By then the Yankees were training full-time at Fort Lauderdale, and we had rented a small apartment on the ocean. Our first morning there we were awakened early, about eight o'clock as I remember, by the phone. It was Helen saying, "Red, is your asking price still the same?" To his answer, "Yes," she replied, "Boy, you've just sold a house." Then came the clincher: "We must have possession by May 15th. The lease on our house expires then." It was then March 1, and we would be in Fort Lauderdale for the full month of spring training, and would have to figure in the time it would take to drive back to New York. I had roughly five weeks in which to find an apartment in New York and make the move from a ten-room house, filled with years of accumulated living. Nils told us later the reason for that surprise early morning phone call. He said, "In all the years Helen and I have been married, it's the only thing she ever asked me for. No fur coats. No expensive trips. Just that house."

My first assignment after our arrival back in New York was again, after twelve years, to find an apartment. There is something to be said for the pressure of time. We took the first thing available that seemed at all suitable. It was in a new building on 51st Street between First Avenue and Beekman Place. The location was perfect. The building was new and the finishing details were still in progress. The apartment we leased was on the eleventh floor at the end of the hall. It consisted of a large living-dining room, two bedrooms, two baths, and a minute pullman kitchen. The second bedroom, which we made into a study, faced south and looked down into the gardens of the brownstone houses on 50th Street and beyond to the United Nations building. It was after we were settled in that we discovered how shoddy the construction of the building was. Soundproofing was practically nonexistent. We knew when the occupants of the apartments above and below us used the plumbing in their bathrooms. For the four-room apartment at 420 East 51st Street we paid forty dollars a month more than we had for the beautiful and spacious apartment at 1035 Fifth Avenue eighteen years before.

Finding the apartment was not as difficult as deciding what to do about the contents of the big house. In what by then were the thirty-two years of our marriage we had always moved from a smaller living space into a larger one. Now we had to consolidate. The getting-rid-of ritual was traumatic. I, being the elder child and having more room, had inherited most of the family memorabilia. What to dispose of, what to keep? Had it not been for the dispose-all we had installed in the basement when we built the house I never would have made it.

There were decisions to be made about the animals. We felt we could keep the two cats in the new small quarters, but not a poodle who sat and cried like a baby when left alone, or a dachshund, named appropriately Miss Willie the piddler. We found country homes for both dogs. It was hard for me to part with the poodle. He had been my companion in many lonely hours, and he loved me jealously.

Then there was all that furniture in all those rooms. What would fit in the apartment, what would we sell, and what would we store for a later day against another move? Finally it was all done, and the movers came to pack. I was so tired that I was only glad to see it ending. It was only after the last piece of furniture came into the apartment, the final barrel of china and glass was unpacked, and the movers left that I looked around and suddenly realized how much of the tangible evidence of thirty-two years of living was gone.

One piece of furniture that went to the warehouse with the moving men had not been intended to go there. Red had bought from Knoll Furniture Company a beautiful custom-made, natural finish birch desk for the house on the Hudson. He loved it, and we had carefully measured (or thought we had). It would crowd the new library, but it could be used. Well, it proved to be too long for the elevator. When turned on its side, it was too tall for the elevator's low ceiling. The mover (by then we had been together so long we seemed like old friends), seeing my husband's disappointed face, offered to take the desk to the roof and try to get it in by crane through the double window in the library. They tried. Unfortunately it just missed clearing the metal window frame. There was nothing to do but send it in the van to the company warehouse to be sold as used furniture. Somebody got quite a bargain.

The couch that had been made to fit in front of the desk stayed with us. It is now in Red's office here in Tallahassee and accommodates an occasional overflow overnight guest. Often when I look at it I see that desk hanging outside the window eleven stories above the New York pavement.

The two-and-a-half years we lived on East 51st Street were not happy ones. Red had not recovered either physically or emotionally from ear surgery, for which he had such high hopes. The fenestration operation to correct certain types of hearing loss was comparatively new but had been quite successful for certain individuals with problems similar to Red's. His surgeon expected a good result. My husband went into surgery with impaired hearing and came out totally deaf in his left ear. Something went wrong and the auditory nerve was destroyed.

Much of Red's work involved interviews and he resented having to explain his deafness. The theater, the opera, and the symphony, all of which he enjoyed, became difficult. I suffered for him and with him. In addition, he was still involved in a slow recovery from a gastrectomy that had been performed while we were still in Scarborough. Being relieved of the many commuting hours either by car or train was a help, but Red hated the confines of the small apartment and the sounds of too close neighbors. My husband is just not a happy apartment dweller.

For me, except for my concern for my husband, it was good to renew my acquaintance with the city I still love. My "odd Friday" concerts were again an easy bus ride or, in bad weather, a short taxi trip. I shall always remember one taxi ride. A Westchester County friend had come in to join me for lunch and the concert. We had a salad in the apartment, then hailed a taxi for the trip across town to the new Symphony Hall. As we were going crosstown through Central Park, traffic came to a complete standstill. There was much honking of horns and great confusion. Our driver left the cab to find the source of the excitement. He came back with a report that something had happened but nobody seemed to know what. We finally reached the hall and were seated hastily. The concert was about to begin. The conductor was on the podium when suddenly a man appeared from the wings. He took the microphone and said, "President Kennedy has just been shot in Dallas. There will be no concert." The audience left in shocked silence.

Living in the city again, I was again free to browse through the art galleries on the East Side, and spend hours in the Museum of Modern Art with the French Impressionists, my favorite painters. During that short second stay of ours in the city, I took an overall course at the New York School of Interior Design. The classes were conducted by a series of well-known persons in the field of decorating. It was informative and interesting, but it was also hard work. They poured on the assignments. I suppose there were fifty students in the course. They came from all parts of the country. Mostly they were people working in the field: owners of furniture stores, textile shops, interior decorators from small towns.

Another pleasant opportunity came about, as best I can recall, by way of a chance encounter at a cocktail party. One of the persons present, an amateur sculptor, told me that she was working in the studio of Harold Castor, whose field was metal sculpture. When I showed interest she offered to take me with her one morning.

Harold and I immediately liked each other. I found his work strong and interesting. When he saw my response he said, "Why don't you come and try your hand?" For about a year I worked along with six or eight other people. It was most informal. Harold was busy with his own commissions but now and then he would come by to see how a student was doing, make a suggestion, change a line perhaps. We moulded in hot black wax and cast in metals—bronze, copper, brass. Mostly we learned by watching Harold work. We have

several Castor pieces in our home here in Tallahassee. One is a strong
Genesis sort of composition. Another is a native dancing girl, which
he did after a Jamaican interlude spent recuperating from pneumonia. Full of primitive rhythm, she is, I think, my favorite. Harold
is a large, strong man physically, and his sculpture looks that way.
He also does lovely soft delicate water colors. Our daughter has one
that he did in Jamaica. The painting is of a native woman holding a
small child.

The end of our second residence in New York was set in motion
with a question asked by my husband. He posed the question over a
second cup of coffee at the breakfast table. I suppose he was feeling
particularly "stir-crazy" in the small apartment. "Lylah," he asked,
"where do you have the most friends?" Willing to play the game,
which was what I presumed it was, I thought of the many friendly
acquaintances we had made through the years in our various moves.
Yet the deepest friendships were those made in my college days and
during the early years of our marriage.

The sorority to which I belonged in college had many members
from Miami. A number of them had gone to New York after graduation. After we moved there from Cincinnati, they formed the nu-
cleus of our social life. Not all of them stayed in New York. Some
returned to Miami, and we would visit again when the broadcasts of
Orange Bowl games at Christmas time found us there. Still later,
when Red was with the Yankees, spring training took us to Miami.
So it was that without much thinking, still playing the game, I responded to my husband's question with "Miami, I suppose."

To my surprise Red said, dead seriously, "Good, let's look for a
house to buy when we are there this spring." That is how we happened to move to Miami.

Red was, of course, busy with baseball. It became my assignment
to find the house. Bob Little, the husband of one of those "college
friends," offered his assistance. Bob was a well-known Miami architect. Several of the buildings on the campus of the University of

Miami are his designs. His work is also represented in several public buildings in the city. Bob made my contact with a realtor. She was a very pleasant, capable woman with unbounded patience. Bob also made me promise we would not make an offer on any house until he had checked its soundness. That promise saved us from making one big mistake.

All of the houses we saw were by appointment and for a specific time. Even now, over fifteen years later, I can't believe some of the places and things the realtor and I saw. Once we were greeted by soiled baby diapers on the coffee table in the living room. I don't know how the rest of the house looked, because we didn't go any further. More than once the homeowner was, at ten o'clock or later, still in her night clothes. Cross, crying babies were routine. I wondered how the homeowners ever expected to sell houses shown under such unattractive conditions. Maybe they didn't really want to sell; moving is a lot of trouble, as I well know.

Finally I found a house that I thought merited asking my busy architect friend to spare the time to check. I had taken Red to see it, and he also found the setup attractive. It was in Coconut Grove, which at that time was a most attractive area of greater Miami. A number of artists and writers lived there, as did some of the older settlers of the city. We felt it would be a congenial atmosphere. The house was a small white cottage of the era when Coconut Grove was a winter resort area for northern retirees. The floors throughout were of lovely Florida hard pine. The house was spotless, and so was its owner, an attractive woman of about my own age.

On the grounds was a large swimming pool with a dressing area. Standing nearby was a charming octagonal guest house consisting of two bedrooms with baths, even a small kitchen. The small house was just right for Red and me. It looked almost like a honeymoon cottage. Sarah, other family members, and friends could come to escape some of the cold northern winters and have their own private quarters in the guest house. I was tired of looking and hoped the quest was ended. Bob Little came for his inspection. He gave a quick look around, then came back to the living room. He stood in the middle of the floor and jumped and landed a few times. The whole floor shook, all the windows rattled. "Let's go," he said, "before it falls down on us." That was how that dream ended.

Red and I had pretty well decided to "wait until next year." The realtor had tried several times to get us to look on Key Biscayne, but we both had been resistant. We had stayed a number of times at the Key Biscayne Hotel and Villas right on the Atlantic Ocean. While it had always been most pleasant, it was completely touristy. Everyone was on holiday. For a home we wanted something that felt more permanent. Our realtor begged. She had located a house on Mashta, the little adjoining island on the bay side.

More to please her than from any real desire to look further, I agreed. She had tried so hard, spent so much of her time; I couldn't say no. The house was "pure developer" but it had beautiful views of Biscayne Bay and Smuggler's Cove, the narrow inlet that separates Mashta Island from Key Biscayne. It was clean. Lovely cool white Cuban tile covered the floors in the living-dining room area and the bedrooms. Bob was called in again. He said, "Lylah, it's sound, I know it is. The architect worked for a while in my office. He is thorough and conscientious, but, my God, it's got no finesse." I replied, "Bob, that's your job. Finesse it into a little Japanese farmhouse." He looked aghast, finally shook his head, and said, "It's a challenge." Fortunately he admired Japanese architecture as much as I had learned to when Red and I were in Japan.

It was the beginning of a very happy relationship. I had heard that Bob was difficult to work with. I never found him so. I respected his skill and training. He had faith in my taste and we got along just fine. Between us, with Red's money, we created something very beautiful. Bob designed a sun deck facing west across the bay. It was a replica of the veranda on one of the temples in Kyoto which I had seen and loved when Red and I were in that Japanese city. Bob and I called it the "Moon Viewing Veranda." It was also great for watching sunsets.

Several years later Bob and I worked together again when he was

the architect for the building of Saint Christopher's Church on Key
Biscayne, and I was a member of the three-person committee set up
to work with him. Again we got along well. He did have trouble with
the rector and I sometimes found myself caught between them as
peacemaker, but Bob and I had no trouble. The little church on Key
Biscayne is a gem, thanks to the artistry of two men, Bob Little, the
architect, and Harold Castor, the sculptor. Castor cast the bronze
altar cross, the pulpit, and the altar rail which tells the story of the
Good Samaritan. If you are ever in the neighborhood, go see Saint
Christopher's. You will find it well worth your time.

PART THREE

HOME AGAIN

KEY BISCAYNE

Red and I bought the house on Key Biscayne in 1965, and at the end of that baseball season we moved in. Spring training in 1966 was no problem. The Yankees trained at Fort Lauderdale and Red commuted by car, an hour's drive. When the season opened he lived in a small suite in the Hilton Hotel in New York. I was alone on Key Biscayne. It was depressing. When I flew to New York in July to spend my sixtieth birthday we decided it would be a good time for me to take that week-long cruise of the Greek islands which I had always dreamed of taking.

We did not know it then, but 1966 was the last year Red would broadcast a full season of major league baseball.

The facts are simple. By 1960, Dan Topping had decided he could run the New York Yankees by himself. He dismissed Casey Stengel, despite Casey's record of ten pennants in twelve years. He let George Weiss, who had been general manager during Stengel's regime, go.

In 1964, Topping fired Mel Allen, who had been the voice of the Yankees since 1946. That year he also dismissed Yogi Berra as manager the day after the Yankees lost the World Series in seven games.

The next season the Yankees collapsed. They fell from first to sixth place in the American League standings, the lowest they had finished in twenty-eight years. The year after that, 1966, they finished last.

Two weeks before the end of the season CBS purchased Topping's remaining shares and named Mike Burke as president. A week later Mike Burke said to Red, "We do not seek to renew your contract."

To me, the Yankees were as cold as the triple-deck mausoleum in which they operated. Red's relationship with them had become uncomfortable well before 1966. His decision to buy the house on Key Biscayne must have been prompted by the growing unease, which also had its impact on his physical health. Now, after more than

Our house at Key Biscayne, Miami.

three decades of life in Cincinnati and New York, we were home again in Florida.

With the help of the pool, in which he swam at least twice and often three times a day, my husband soon regained his health. The five-days-a-week broadcasts on WGBS which he did by microphone from the desk in his office were just enough to keep him from missing too much the years of intense activity of play-by-play baseball broadcasting. I grew orchids. The climate on Mashta Island was perfect for them. I learned how to buy plants so that I always had some in bloom. When we sold the house well over a hundred plants went to the new owners.

We also were free, for the first time in our married years, to take long vacations whenever we chose. For years Red had said that the first summer he was free of a baseball schedule he would buy a new automobile and drive to see the Rocky Mountains. It was a boyhood dream. Well, he did. He bought a shiny dark green Lincoln Continental—I selected the color—and in the summer of 1967 we started out with only four hundred miles on the odometer. By this time Red was writing a weekly column for the Sunday Miami *Herald*. We stopped in cities along the way where he did a series of interviews for the columns which he sent back to the paper.

Our first stop was in Tampa where he interviewed Al Lopez, the great Hall of Fame catcher, who was newly retired as manager of the Chicago White Sox. In Atlanta he visited with Bobby Dodd, longtime coach of Georgia Tech. Red wanted very much to have an interview with the great golfer Bobby Jones, who was then in failing health and would not permit himself to be interviewed in person. Dodd, a close friend of the ailing golfer, arranged a telephone interview and Jones was most cordial.

When we reached Chicago, by lucky chance both the White Sox and the Cubs were in town to play a scheduled exhibition game. Red

Swimming pool at Key Biscayne house.

was able to interview the two managers. Leo Durocher was now with the Cubs and Eddie Stanky had recently replaced Al Lopez as manager with the White Sox. Both men were good friends from the Brooklyn Dodger days. It was like old times. I began to feel as though I were on a business trip with a roving reporter.

After the last interview we headed straight west for Yellowstone National Park. We drove, for what seemed endless miles, through the farmlands of Iowa and Nebraska into the beautiful, wrongly called Bad Lands of South Dakota. We saw the Rockies, the Grand Tetons, and the Craters of the Moon. We spent the fourth of July in Salt Lake City. We heard an organ recital in the Tabernacle and saw a production of the play *The Coming of the Mormons*. I remember being impressed by how clean the city was. Even the streets looked cleanly swept.

Our plan had always been to return to Florida by the southern route through the Indian country of Arizona and New Mexico. A look at the map showed us how close we were to Las Vegas. Being by nature curious we decided to have a look at the gambling capital of the United States. We made a three-day reservation at Caesar's Palace. In the middle of the desert, not far north of Las Vegas, the air conditioning on the new Lincoln went out. We arrived in town hot and cross. Before checking in at the hotel, we spent an hour or so at a garage getting the ailing air conditioning fixed. It was not an auspicious introduction to the city. The heat was oppressive.

We had not come to Las Vegas to gamble, only to observe. When Red began his career as a sports broadcaster he made a pact with himself never to gamble, not even so much as for a Coca-Cola. He felt, and rightly, that with a betting interest in the outcome of an event, objectivity disappeared. As for myself, I am much too fond of a sure outcome to risk money on a roll of the dice.

When we checked in at the hotel desk the action was going full tilt. The tables were crowded with customers standing in line to claim any vacated chairs. There was no background music, unless the constant clatter of slot machines can be considered such. It was aesthetically unattractive. Our room was luxurious with a fine view of the activity around the mammoth pool. It was not as crowded as the lobby had been.

We attended the dinner show. I remember how crowded in we were. There was no privacy, just those long rows of narrow tables facing the stage. I admit the view of the show was excellent, even for five-foot-tall Lylah, but oh, that elbow intimacy with strangers. Milton Berle had star billing, and he was excellent, a great showman. He was raw in spots, but the audience loved it. I understand his supper show had an R rating. He was very generous to Red, acknowledging his presence in a friendly, complimentary fashion. We all like to be recognized.

On our second night we went for dinner to another hotel. The star performer there took his little daughter—I would guess she was five or six years old—on stage with him. He sang to her one of the hit songs of the day, "More Than You'll Ever Know." His voice and presentation were suited to the song. It was sentimental and touching, but I kept wondering about his little daughter. Maybe she loved it and grew up to be a star in her own right. Red and I had felt differently about our daughter. We tried hard to keep Sarah from being exploited by her father's professional success.

When we got back to Caesar's Palace late in the evening the tables and slot machines were still going strong. We agreed that we had seen enough and left an early wake-up call at the desk. When we checked out at eight Sunday morning, there were already, or perhaps still, players at the tables and machines. The few chairs and benches in the lobby were occupied by occasional nappers. My final reaction to Las Vegas was "how sad, how empty."

We broke the long hot summers on Key Biscayne with other trips. We revisited Mexico, which we both love, and discovered the beautiful colonial city of Morelia. Our daughter had built a mountain cabin in Keene Valley in the Adirondacks and we spent time there in September when she would be back teaching in New York. She would come up for occasional weekends, and we had a chance to visit. September was a good time to be away from Miami. It was hurricane season there.

Twice, after Red was no longer bound by the schedule of play-by-play baseball broadcasting, we spent leisurely spring vacations in Provence and on the French Riviera. It was a delight to see the actual countryside my favorite artists painted so beautifully. We flew to Paris and from there took the Mistral, that marvelous luxury train, from Paris to Nice. Red was at that time broadcasting short spots five days a week for radio station WGBS in Miami. He took a Sony tape recorder to France and sent cassettes back for broadcast material. The sponsor was the Mercedes dealers of Miami. It was just the right amount of work. Red did little vignettes of sights and scenes that struck our fancy. Sometimes it would be a dialogue between the two of us, commenting on what we had seen or done. It was fun and left plenty of time for whatever we wished to do.

In Vence we visited the chapel in the Dominican convent where Matisse did the Stations of the Cross, in black lines on white tiles. For the window panes he used joyous blues and yellows. Several years later we were again in Vence. It was Good Friday and when the chapel was opened to the public after the twelve-to-three meditations we were there. What a way to observe Good Friday! Matisse was an old man, almost eighty, when he decorated the chapel.

In Arles we saw the Roman arena dating back to the second century A.D.—no gladiators there now, nor Christians and lions, but we were told there are still bullfights during the season. We went out to Saint-Remy to the hospital where the poor tortured painter Van Gogh committed himself for treatment. The room in which he was confined was, in actuality, a cell. There is a heavy iron bolt on the door, with a tiny peephole above through which the sick epileptic artist was watched. It was not long after his stay at Saint-Remy that Van Gogh shot himself, thus ending his torture.

We went to Avignon to see the big Picasso exhibit at the Palace of the Popes. I was not impressed or particularly stirred. For me there was too much of his grotesque distortion of the human form. The room housing his erotica distressed me. It was not sexually stimulating, only ugly. Forgive me my amateur's review of the exhibit. I wonder how those long-gone popes would have regarded it. I found the recent Picasso show at the Museum of Modern Art in New York, in 1980, quite another thing. It was a magnificent outpouring of a great artist's work.

That Easter vacation in Provence was mighty near perfect, not a cloud, just golden sunshine and the perfume of roses in bloom everywhere. Easter afternoon we decided to drive up in the hills to Grasse, where much of the French perfume and soap is made. On the way we were passed by a large truck completely loaded with (can you believe it?) just rose petals. I suppose they were on their way to one of the factories. As the driver accelerated to pass us on a hill we were showered with rose petals. What a country. I have often said, only half facetiously, "Never mind heaven, just send me to Provence." I would go back tomorrow.

TALLAHASSEE: HOME AGAIN

During the six years we lived on Key Biscayne the island underwent many changes. It boomed. The ocean side of the island began to look like Miami Beach. It was fast becoming a solid expanse of hotels and condominiums. The southern tip of the island, which had been declared a state park when Rickenbacker Causeway was completed, was still natural and quiet, but on weekends and in summer when the children of Miami were out of school it began to resemble Coney Island.

Our own little Mashta Island was changing. There was much building going on. Large, expensive year-round homes were being built by wealthy retirees from the north and the Midwest. We lost our view of Smuggler's Cove to several of them. A "For Sale" sign went up on the land across the road from our Moon Viewing Veranda and the bay.

The handwriting was on the wall. Besides, we had begun to grow restless in the land of eternal summer and sun. We missed the change of seasons. We certainly did not yearn for the long hard winters of New York, but, increasingly, we did feel the need for some cool weather.

It was Red who said, "Lylah, you often talk of how happy you were in Tallahassee in your college years, how you loved the spring there with its explosion of camellias, dogwoods, azaleas, and roses. When we go to Sarah's cabin in New York this summer, why don't we drive by Tallahassee and take a look around?" We did.

It was as simple as that. We looked in a casual sort of way for two days—Saturday and Sunday. Actually we were more interested in getting a feeling for the town than anything else. Ryals Lee, a realtor, showed us a few houses, but nothing struck our fancy. Sunday night after dinner we discussed the impressions of our two days, shrugged our shoulders, and said, "Oh well, another summer."

There was no pressure on us. We were well settled in Key Biscayne.

We were in our motel room getting settled for the night when Ryals called to say a decision had been reached that afternoon by the owner of a house which had never been shown. The owner had decided to put it on the market Monday morning. The realtor thought it was the sort of thing we were looking for, because it was in excellent condition and was less than a year old. We were not very interested. Our thoughts were much more on making an early start and getting to Sarah's cabin in the Adirondacks. We finally agreed that if we could take a look no later than nine in the morning, okay.

When we arrived at nine sharp the owner, Mrs. Fanny Rosenberg, was ready for us. So was the house. She was elderly, well dressed in a handsome green pants suit which was becoming to her reddish blonde hair. She had coffee and sweet rolls of her own making waiting for us on the breakfast room table. Mrs. Rosenberg was cordial, and explained to us that her husband had died a few months before. The house was now too big for her, and, besides, she was afraid to live in it alone. It was obviously new. Mrs. Rosenberg had not even finished hanging curtains in all of the rooms. It was also spotless and sturdy. However, what really sold me was that it sat in a grove of pine trees. I counted them: twenty-five. In among them was an ancient live oak. To achieve such majesty it must have been growing there long before I was born. Ah, nostalgia.

Red and I proed-and-conned all the way from Tallahassee to Greenville, South Carolina. By the time we reached the motel in a driving rainstorm, we had come to a decision. We telephoned to Tallahassee and made an offer. There were a few details to be spelled out, but by the time our visit in the Adirondacks was finished the house was ours. I flew from Miami once, for the routine checking for fit of carpets and furniture. No more oversized desks.

On January 10, 1972, we packed our overnight bags, loaded ourselves and the two cats in the car and started for our new home. The six years in the sun were finished. Our last stop before hitting the Sunshine Parkway was at our vet's. He gave each cat a tranquilizer

shot and promised us a quiet journey. Mama cat Bella curled up
between Red's feet and slept most of the time. Esau, her son, howled
every mile and minute of the way.

The moving van arrived the next day. The crew was a couple of
days moving in the furniture, unloading the barrels of china, silver,
and pots, and hanging clothes in closets. David, the foreman, was
great. When I would start looking for some special treasure and grow
into a frantic fear that it was lost, he would say, "It's here, Mrs.
Barber." It always was. He was as gently reassuring as a mother
soothing an overwrought child.

Alice came to help us put things away. She had done housework
for friends of ours on Key Biscayne until her mother in Tallahassee
had become ill. Then she came back home to care for her and an
invalid brother. She came regularly once a week to help me until her
mother and brother both died and she could go back to Miami.

Finally, it was all done. The last barrel was back in the van. Alice
had made the beds and departed for the day. The cats were happily
sniffing the strange trees and bushes in the yard. Red and I were
finally in our new home. He made a pitcher of martinis and we sat
down to enjoy the quiet.

Tallahassee has been good to us. Much has changed. It is a city
now, not the small town it was in my college days. The college of a
thousand young women that I loved is now a university of over
twenty-five thousand coed students. I can't find my way around the
campus. There is a football team.

Red and I were not long in realizing how many ties we had with
Tallahassee. One of our first visitors was Annie Sensabaugh. She and
I had gone through training at Riverside Hospital together. At college we were two of the three candidates for the first B.S. degrees in
nursing ever given at Florida State College for Women. Annie
brought the traditional gifts of bread and salt to ensure good fortune
in a new home. Dr. William Hudson Rogers, under whom I had a
course in Browning's poetry my senior year, was still living. He
and Mrs. Rogers asked me to their home for morning coffee. Jerry

Carter, with whom Red shared an apartment while a student at the University of Florida, dropped by with his wife. We had never met her, but she greeted us with an armload of azalea blossoms. Rainey Cawthon (we both knew him while I was working at the university infirmary in Gainesville) came by with his wife Sarah. Lee Graham, the rector of Saint John's Church, made a parochial call. His wife Betty is the daughter of Dr. Thomas, for whom I had worked when I first went, as a bride, to live in Gainesville. Betty was one of Dr. Thomas' twin adolescent daughters. Mrs. Rosenberg's daughter, Evelyn Block, called early with a Tallahassee bouquet of camellias. She and Al, her husband, became our good friends. It was all very warm and Southern. We quickly felt at home. It was the environment in which we had grown up.

As soon as spring came we turned our efforts to creating a garden under the pine trees. We went to the Tallahassee Nursery and met the young owner, Gene Ellis. Gene understood that we had neither the time nor the patience to wait for young plants to mature. He found, and moved in for us, two large southern magnolia trees. They screen our front yard from the street traffic. Ligustrum and redtop hedges gave us quick privacy. We planted azaleas and camellias where they like to grow, under the pine trees. Red added a banana shrub that he recalled from his boyhood in Mississippi. Several years later we steeled ourselves, uprooted five pine trees, and put in a replacement for Red's Key Biscayne fountain of youth, a small oval pool. At the far end, for a formal touch, we placed five cypress trees to remind us of happy days in Provence. An English lead figure of a young girl holding a bird in her hand stands in front of the center cypress.

As I write these last words a mockingbird outside my window is selling a bill of goods to his lady love.

In my lifetime I have played my part in the creation of five gardens. I still miss the lilac and rhododendron of my northern gardens. The orchids of Key Biscayne were exotic and beautiful but . . . I love most my Tallahassee garden.

In the six years we lived in Miami on Key Biscayne, we often took short holidays on the Keys and watched them change from the wild, quiet beauty of our first sight into what was becoming almost an extension of Miami Beach.

In 1980 Red had a speaking engagement in the Fort Lauderdale area. Since we were close by we decided to go on to Miami and the Keys. It was at the height of the Cuban boat lift, and we were interested to see what effect the influx of the refugees would have on Key West. Since it was also the height of the summer tourist season we felt it wise to make reservations ahead. We were surprised that we not only were able to get accommodations at the Pier House Inn (built around the Custom House, one of the oldest buildings in Key West) but also the room we wanted, overlooking the harbor. The traffic driving down was light. We did pass a number of old dilapidated buses heading toward Miami. They were crowded, and we assumed that the occupants were refugees being taken to Miami for processing. When we reached town the streets were almost deserted; the inn was uncrowded, and the shops were empty. The townspeople who depended upon tourists for their livelihood were crying. People who had seen and heard the news on television had become frightened and had cancelled. The harbor, seen from our balcony, was quiet. There were a few Coast Guard boats heading out to sea in the early morning. The pleasure boats came in to anchor for the night, but otherwise the harbor was empty. Actually, the refugee boats were docked at the old naval station where the people were loaded on to buses and sent to Miami. The whole operation was strictly "offbase."

We stayed two days, said our farewells to Key West, and headed for home. Since Tallahassee is in northwest Florida, we decided to take the Tamiami Trail to Naples and go up the West Coast. It was forty-one years since we had made our first trip across the Trail. We were curious to see how it had changed.

Everything was different. The modern highway cut the time in two, and we were grateful. But, there were phony Indian villages with gasoline pumps. There were stores filled with cheap moccasins and ugly Seminole blouses and skirts. They were obviously made by machine in the factory area of Miami, probably, ironically, by Cuban refugee labor. Fast-food shacks waited for the tourists' money. The birds were few and the peace was gone.

However, on the other side of the coin, there is a new road that goes through the Glades. It runs seventy-six miles, straight as an Indian's arrow, and it is called "Alligator Alley." Because it is a toll road with limited access and is crossed only once by a narrow secondary road leading north from Ochokee to Immokalee, it is untouched by commercialism. There are no gas pumps. When we took it a few years ago, shortly after it opened, the tall cypress trees which shed their needles in the short Florida winter were just beginning to put out a few tentative pale green needles. The gray trunks were festooned with brilliant scarlet bromeliads. There were many birds, and it was beautiful.

In the fall of 1980 Red and I drove from Tallahassee to Jackson, Mississippi, to spend Thanksgiving with his sister Virginia. I saw on the map that our route from Montgomery to Jackson led straight through Selma and across the bridge that Martin Luther King made famous, or perhaps infamous, in 1965 in his drive for civil rights for blacks. My memory flashed back to that day. We were living in New York, and in those troubled days we Southerners were taking something of a beating from our northern liberal friends. I had been so proud to see and point out to our friends LeRoy Collins, former governor of my state of Florida, marching with King across that bridge. One of the special pleasures of living in Tallahassee was becoming friends with LeRoy and Mary Call Collins. Governor Collins' heroic walk across that bridge at Selma with Martin Luther King cost him dearly when he ran for the United States Senate against Ed Gurney.

As we were approaching the outskirts of Selma, needing gasoline, we stopped at a filling station. The attendant at the pump looked as unkempt as his rundown enterprise. When Red returned from his futile search of the building he said to the attendant, "My friend,

In New York City to spend our fiftieth anniversary with Sarah.

you don't have any restrooms?" "Oh, yeah, they are just around the side of the building." "But," replied Red, "they both have signs saying 'Out of Order.'" The reply, at three o'clock in the afternoon, was, "I just ain't gotten around to takin' 'em off." When I told Red what I guessed was the probable reason for the dodge—to keep out blacks—he replied, "Considering the condition of the facility, I think his fears of contamination are unfounded."

"The more things change, the more they remain the same."

In the spring of 1981 my husband and I returned to New York to celebrate our fiftieth wedding anniversary with our daughter Sarah, who is an English professor at La Guardia Community College, part of the City University of New York. We had spent twenty-eight of the fifty years of our marriage either in Manhattan itself or in the commuting towns of Scarsdale and Scarborough, and loved the area. This was where we wanted to be.

We found a changed city. The beautiful mansions of the late 1800s and early 1900s along Fifth Avenue and Park Avenue in which I had delighted had been largely replaced by the sterile monolithic towers of glass that seemed to shut out the sky. The canyons in between were choked with people. The corner chestnut roasters were outnumbered by portable fast-food bars, busy cooking hamburgers and hot dogs for the office workers pouring out of those glass towers for their lunch break.

All kinds of people sat on the steps of St. Thomas' Church at 53rd and Fifth. Some were eating their lunch. Others, derelicts of the great city, sat there as though they had no other place to go. We had heard about the "bag ladies of New York." They were there.

The beautiful shops and art galleries were there, too. The elegant, expensive restaurants were crowded and the food was superb. The hard times of New York, however, were also there for those who wished to see. Once, after an evening at the theater in the Broadway area of the Forties, we made the mistake of walking to Eighth Avenue in search of a taxi. It was frightening—doorways filled with people asleep or passed out from drink or drugs.

Yes, there were changes, not all of them happy, but two things remained unchanged. We went into Tiffany's to get a repair on a ring that had been bought there years ago. The clerks were just as arrogantly patronizing as they had been fifty years before.

And, on Sunday when we attended service at St. Thomas', the church was packed, the music beautiful, and the choir boys still looked and sang like angels.

BETWEEN THE TREES

When I was a small child, after my father died, Mother sent me to Lake City to spend summers with Grandma Scarborough. Mother had to work. I was almost without roots. But not quite. Grandma had love and warmth. She gave me the first real security I knew. Also, Grandma had a fig tree.

When the figs were ripe she would let me climb the tree. In fact, she assured me it was a high privilege to climb and pick and get the sticky milk-juice on my hands.

I look back some seventy years to trace a happiness and a safety to a fig tree in Grandma's side yard in downtown Lake City. Today that yard is a parking lot. The fig tree fell to a devouring bulldozer.

The other morning at breakfast Red and I had preserved figs. They were made by Mildred Holmes, Uncle Fred's second wife, who after his death remarried and remained in Lake City. Mildred has a fig tree in her yard, and it stands and bears not far from the one I used to climb and harvest at Grandma's.

I looked at the small brown preserved figs from Mildred's tree and I thought about the one I used to climb—the one that was cut down so that automobiles could park on sterile asphalt. I realized the distance from the tree of my childhood to Mildred's is about four blocks, and that Lake City itself is only a hundred miles due east on I-10. Two easy hours. And yet between the two trees are countless miles and seven decades of time—an odyssey with one fig tree marking a child's security and another one connoting a full maturity.

I go to New York from here. I have sailed around South America from here. I have driven to Mexico from here. I have traveled to take passage on the Alaskan Waterway from here.

Now, each year, Mildred sends her figs. A talisman of where I was born, almost from the very spot of North Florida soil. From Grandma's tree to Mildred's.

"And Judah and Israel lived in security—each under his own vine and under his own fig tree . . . " (1 Kings 4:25).